SEVEN SACRED TRUTHS

Also by Wanda John-Kehewin

In the Dog House

Published by Talonbooks

SEVEN SACRED TRUTHS

Poems

Wanda John-Kehewin

Talonbooks

To Pamela,
may you know
your light shines
bright
and that
everything will
be OK.
Peace, love &
light

Talonbooks
278 East First Avenue, Vancouver, British Columbia, Canada v5T 1A6
talonbooks.com

Talonbooks is located on xʷməθkʷəy̓əm, Sḵwx̱wú7mesh, and səl̓ilwətaʔɬ Lands.

First printing: 2018

Typeset in Arno
Printed and bound in Canada on 100% post-consumer recycled paper

Interior and cover design by Typesmith
Cover illustration #1 "vertebrae" by Mónica Leitão Mota via Flickr (CC 2.0)
Cover illustration #2 "girl" by 정선 박 (o_lie) via Flickr (CC 2.0)

Talonbooks gratefully acknowledges the financial support of the Canada Council for the Arts, the Government of Canada through the Canada Book Fund, and the Province of British Columbia through the British Columbia Arts Council and the Book Publishing Tax Credit.

LIBRARY AND ARCHIVES CANADA CATALOGUING IN PUBLICATION

John-Kehewin, Wanda, 1971–, author
    Seven sacred truths : poems / Wanda John-Kehewin.

ISBN 978-1-77201-213-2 (SOFTCOVER)

    I. Title.

PS8619.O4455S48 2018   C811'.6   C2018-903151-4

Dedicated to my children, my life.

Contents

SEVEN SACRED TRUTHS

The Seven Sacred Truths

1. To value knowledge and to teach others is to know WISDOM. My entire life has been learning and it still continues to be a learning process. Most times have been about learning the hard way. Growing up, I was a very analytical child. I watched the world around me. It was by far not a perfect world, but a world filled with shame, distrust, sadness, depression, hopelessness, hatred, destruction of the spirit. Sometimes the world we live in is flawed. We have to take off our destructive blinders to see it. Reaching out to others in the community to help us on our path of healing is not a weakness, but a strength. The journey isn't easy but it is going to be way easier than hating yourself every day, especially if the same mistakes are made over and over.

    Wisdom is knowing when to stop doing something, or when to tell others to stop, when to ask for help, when to pray, when to call a friend, when to cry, when to protect yourself, when to protect others, even when to sleep. The golden key to wisdom is to take a lesson learned and apply it forward in every aspect of your life and stand in your truth. Sometimes, some lessons take a longer time to learn, especially coming from generations of dysfunction brought about by the disease of colonization.

    Wisdom is learning and never thinking that we are better than anyone else. Wisdom is realizing that every single human being in this world is the same and that one day we are all going to leave this world, and that is the only constant.

    Wisdom is knowing that we are going to leave this world and that we never know when, so we must live in each and every moment like it is a precious gift, because it is – a gift so that we may, at the end of our lives, know we have tried our very best to heal and to pass on that healing to future generations of hurting humans.

    Wisdom is surrendering to the human condition where wars live, where hatred lives, racism exists, classism is alive. The ego is at the base of society's downfall and of realizing that this physical body is temporary and so is every other material thing that the human condition hangs onto. The spirit lives on and is trying to survive alongside our physical being. The spirit is the wisdom and, through our spirit, we can go beyond the human condition. We are all interconnected, but it is so hard to see this if we are not able to distinguish the difference between the physical body and the true essence of ourselves, which has no words, no physical form, and is absolute.

2. To know LOVE is to know harmony with Mother Earth, earth family, friends, animals, nature, and self, which is not the physical body. Love takes on many forms. It could be the love between mother and child, father and child, grandmother and child, friend and friend (kinship ties), the love for animals, the love of this very planet that we depend on for survival. Last but not least, the love between two people who choose to be together and who complement each other and do not hinder each other in any way, but who push each other with love and kindness in the right direction.

To know love beyond the constraints of the human condition is to know true freedom. Domestic violence is not love but shows that there is a need for unconditional love that was never there to begin with. To realize that love is not a thing but a feeling which shows you what you are committed to. If you truly love another person, there should be no reason to hurt another person. A lot of people are lost in what they think is love, but are actually just with someone not to feel alone.

Loving yourself first as you are and knowing you have every right to walk this Earth as everyone else does is the beginning of healing. To know you were perfect from day one, and to also know that the "bad stuff" that happened to you does not have to define who you are now. The past is not who you are and is only a marker of where you have been. To truly know love for yourself is to be comfortable in your human form and to strive to help others do the same. Even one kind sentence can change someone's view of themselves. Words can empower. They can also destroy.

Love is not destroying another person nor destroying Mother Earth or all her creatures and living things. Love is taking only what you need and sharing the rest. In a world full of competition and consumerism, this can be a hard concept.

3. To honour every living creature, living being, including yourself, is to have RESPECT. Respect was not something that I was familiar with growing up. I knew what it was supposed to mean but it eluded me while I was in foster care. It eluded me while my people and family were struggling to make sense of the changing world around us, while still trying to heal from the tidal wave of colonialism. I knew the word and I knew what it was supposed to mean, but if it isn't part of your life, how can you truly know the deeper meaning?

I had to learn respect from others outside of my family and community, as they were just surviving. I grew up knowing what respect meant but it wasn't until I was older and well on my path to healing that it made any sense. How could I understand what respect meant if I didn't even know how to respect myself?

How was I going to respect myself if it wasn't taught to me or shown to me? I had to learn the hard way and a lot of times it was my spirit that showed me. I would do things like drink way too much and do things while under the influence that affected my spirit. I would know I was harming myself because my spirit would feel empty, sad, lost. It was the community that I had built around myself and my spirit that showed me what respect was.

When I was respecting myself, my spirit would feel at peace. When I was harming my physical, spiritual, emotional, and mental well-being, my spirit would let me know. I would feel alone, lost, empty, and I felt a void I thought I needed another person to fill. My spirit was one of my main teachers.

Just because I grew up and felt disrespect to my entire being did not mean that I could not learn respect. It has been a long journey, not an easy one, but a journey so well worth it. Respect can be learned through others who are respectful toward you, and it is your spirit who will let you know when something doesn't feel right.

Respect in its truest sense comes from feeling connected to others, yourself (spirit), animals, and Mother Earth. Respect for yourself, your body, your spirit, your emotions, your thoughts is key to acceptance of the self. Acceptance of the self allows us to be in the moment, to enjoy what is going on around us instead of living in the past or looking too far in the future.

Respect is making sure to honour other beings and living creatures around us and not taking more than we can use, especially if it means someone else is suffering because of our actions.

4. COURAGE is to face the self, others, and conflict with integrity. Courage is feeling and acknowledging what your spirit is trying to tell you so that it can protect you. Honour yourself and spirit by listening and following it. That is courage.

Courage is standing up for those who cannot stand up for themselves, like children, animals, and Mother Earth. Growing up I lacked courage because I did not recognize it. I did not even know what courage was. I knew what the word was, but its meaning was abstract in my life. Courage to me was to run away from everything that I felt was a threat to my physical, spiritual, emotional, and mental well-being. Running is not the answer. I left "home" at fourteen and went to the big city; left Edmonton, Alberta, at nineteen and moved to Vancouver, British Columbia, because I was running from my past. What I did not realize was that just because I came running to British Columbia, it didn't mean I could run from my past.

As a child, I had been abused sexually, physically, mentally, and emotionally. I had to learn to love myself and to accept me as I was and as I am. Some days, I still have to practice loving myself because those taped messages in my head from my past that tell me "I'm not good enough" sneak up on me. Realizing that those are "tapes" I don't need anymore and will not be a slave to anymore makes the difference between me just surviving and me living.

It took courage to search for people who would not hurt me and sometimes I made mistakes and thought I was in love and had finally found what I had been searching for, when really I had walked into a violent relationship and mistook abuse for love. I mistook jealousy for a powerful love, which was not the case. It took courage to ask for help to walk away. Everyone around me growing up was surviving, and just because we are surviving does not mean we are living or courageous.

Courage is dealing with the things that have hurt you in the past in a constructive way and not masking it with addiction or suppression. Courage is creating a safe space for yourself to heal. Courage is reaching out to others for help. Help is available. Just because I see a counsellor does not mean anything is wrong with me. It means I have the courage to uncover the truth, to work at putting things in perspective so they make sense to me.

Courage is working through those things that happened in the past so that your perspective changes. Then you can help others by modelling courage, sharing with others the hardships you have overcome so that they may also take that first step toward healing. To do the healing work takes courage. It is easy to hide behind addiction, especially if you don't even know there's something wrong to begin with. You just know that you are always chasing something but you can never figure out what it is. Jumping from relationship to relationship seems to be a telltale sign of trying to fill that void.

Courage is going beyond the comfort zone and discovering why we choose ways to fill that void that disempowers our spirit, which then disempowers our entire being.

5. HONESTY means being grounded in your words and being true to yourself. Those voices in our heads that say "I am not good enough" or "I can do this all alone, I don't need anyone," aren't from our spirit. In order to honour ourselves and be honest with ourselves, we must figure out where these internal messages come from.

All along, we were always good enough, we were always meant to be loved and loving, we were always meant to be respected and respecting, always meant to be courageous, always meant to be humble, always meant to be true and honest to ourselves, always meant to learn and also to teach (Wisdom). Somewhere along the line, humanity has become so disconnected that our interconnectedness has been damaged, to the point that it is no longer common knowledge or practice that WE ARE CONNECTED.

6. HUMILITY is to know yourself as being connected to everyone and everything living and breathing on Mother Earth, and respecting those lives and beings.

    Humility is being able to walk in your own shoes and in others' shoes with no distinction of differences.

    Humility is being able to cry and pray for yourself and others in ways that honour their lives and yours.

    Humility is overcoming the ego and all its flaws, and realizing that the constructs of ego is the human condition. It is constant work to be humble and have humility, especially in the world that is now full of disconnectedness, where others are shaming others.

    Humility is sometimes being quiet when someone is crying, and just listening without offering any advice unless they ask.

7. TRUTH is to know interconnectedness and to never question it. Truth is to work toward sharing that message through actions and words and empowering others through those actions and words. Language is powerful.

    Truth is knowing and being the Seven Sacred Truths. It is not always easy because we are in the "human condition" in a world that is so disconnected and so far removed from the spiritual and the spirit.

Creator, Universe, Ancestors, Mother Earth

Please help us come into this circle with open minds, ears, and hearts and

the wisdom to allow us to use our words each and every day in ways that

benefit our friends, our family, and even our people we just meet

so that we may make a difference to those around us in ways that they need most.

May we have the gentleness of heart for others and ourselves so that we may

overcome the human condition with strength, grace, beauty, compassion, and love.

Help us to forgive and learn to forgive so that we may model forgiveness and faith

for our friends, our family, strangers, and especially for those who are suffering around us

so that they may also see the beauty that is abundant through Mother Earth and spirit.

Help us so that we may model for others the lightness of heart and the strength

to go on that comes with healing and forgiveness and to be able to be that role model

of healing, lightness, and strength to others suffering in silence and suffering alone.

May we lend courage to those who need a gentle push, a hug, or a kind word.

May we put all judgments aside and remember we are all connected and the same.

May we remember we all have the right to walk this earth in truth, freedom, and dignity,

just as everybody else regardless of race or class, nothing less and nothing more.

Creator, Universe, Ancestors, Mother Earth

Please help our brothers, our sisters, our grandmothers, our grandfathers, and our children

who are suffering from addiction, disease, depression, sadness, hopelessness.

May you walk with them side by side and embrace them in your arms

as they walk on their path; may you bring them lightness of heart, peace of mind,

and the ability to let the past rest and journey to a better today and hopeful tomorrow.

Please remind them the past is not who they are but only where they have been.

A place travelled that they never need to go to again except in sharing with others

the ways out of addiction, disease, depression, sadness, hopelessness, and

to also share that when you are at the end of your rope, there is hope

through the sharing of story, the sharing of experience, and living beyond judgment.

Creator, Universe, Ancestors, Mother Earth

Please help all the living creatures: the four-leggeds, the winged ones,

the finned ones, the ones that crawl next to Mother Earth.

Please embrace them in your arms and help them to adjust to this world

where humans are changing their homes, their minds, and their lives.

Help them continue to be in great numbers and to find safe homes, good food, and clean water.

Please help them, **Creator, Universe, Ancestors, and Mother Earth.**

Creator, Ancestors, Universe

Please help Mother Earth who is being ravaged, pillaged, and crucified.

Help the two-leggeds realize the destruction of Mother Earth travels forward,

destroying their own Mother's home, as well as the other creatures who are struggling to survive.

Help the two-leggeds gather together one day soon to protect their precious Mother

and to be a role model of that relationship that was always meant to be harmonious:

Mother and children, a duality of harmony, one beating heart, like it was meant to be.

Give us the courage, wisdom, love, humility, respect, honesty, and truth to do this.

Creator, Universe, Ancestors, Mother Earth

Help us to be mindful and to remember to be thankful for the small things in life that grace

us each and every day like the food on our tables, the water we drink and bathe in,

the smiles from our children, our friends that are like our families, the knowledge,

and the thoughts that turn to action when we think outside ourselves and think of others.

May we change our children's lives for future generations so that when our children look back

and think of us through the Seven Sacred Truths, they will know the Seven Sacred Truths, and will

also want to pave the road for their children and their children's children and Mother Earth

who breathes life into all things, our Mother is slowly dying for us, tangles in her hair.

Thank you, **Creator, Universe, Ancestors, Mother Earth,** for the love we feel when

we are with our families and for the love we feel when we are gathered in circles

and we are of one heart, one mind and one direction – casting aside ego.

Thank You. Thank you. Thank you.

Pretty and **Pink** with New Shoes

Since I was six I have respected the rain. A love that surpasses even the
love of myself. The rain rests on my face and I know I am. Splishy, splashy,
exalted rain. I know there is life, love, and buffalo bones. Given to me by
dead relatives who want to be vindicated. Fate may allow me to have that
vindication I see resonating on anyone and everyone who has not been
kicked in the past so hard your future children fell. Colonization killed my
mom, you know. Splishy, splashy, exalted pain. I know there is life, love, and
buffalo bones. Given to me by dead relatives who want to be vindicated.
I was raised on a poverty-stricken reservation. The dogs, my family, and the
trees my witnesses. Splishy, splashy, exalted sane. Surrounded by Sweetgrass,
and bibles treading heavily with cast-off shoes. Hand-me-downs from pink
kids getting new ones every season change. Like tires. I know there is life,
love, and buffalo bones. Given to me by dead relatives who want to be
vindicated. I was planted in the foster system at seven and hopefully I would
grow into a beneficial Indian. Splishy, splashy, exalted disdain. I was seven
and I wanted to be pretty and **Pink** with new shoes. I know there is life, love,
and buffalo bones. Given to me by dead relatives who want to be vindicated.
My mother was buried in the rain. The rain rests on her coffin and I know she
was. Splishy, splashy, exalted, and slain. Rain always reminds me of her tears.
God's tears Mom said but she is dead. And I know at least two beings are
crying for her. Splishy, splashy, exalted vein. I was terrified by how beautiful
the stained glass was and how tall the steeple. Using my hands, I still see
all the people. When I grew up I would always be in awe and frightened by
stained glass in the house of the Lord. Splishy, splashy, exalted pane. I know
there is life, love, and buffalo bones. Given to me by dead relatives who want
to be vindicated. A woman's period was a sacred thing. That was the Indian
way. I can instill this in my daughters even if the tape in my head plays over
and over, dirty, dirty, dirty. I try to make a new tape, **Fuck you**, **Fuck you**,
Fuck you. Splishy, splashy, exalted brain. The day I charge five dollars for a
poem and I don't get paid is the day I'm either in love or I am dead. Splishy,
splashy, exalted refrain. I know there is life, love, and buffalo bones. Given to
me by dead relatives who want to be vindicated.

Mortal Spirit Angel

Daughter
Sunny, blameless
Sentient, smiling, loving
Pickpocket of my healing heart
Angel

Angel
Sinless, helpless
Dreaming, helping, guarding
A gift to save me from myself
Saviour

Saviour
Hero, altruist, crucial
Saving, freeing, ridding
A cleansing of a ruthless past
Spirit

Spirit
Essence, wholeness, being
Searching, finding, exposed
A dispatcher of forgiveness
Human

Human
Sadness, gladness
Crying, laughing, finding
Soul journey purpose
Mortal Spirit

Coyote Crying

The day she called – the smell of burning sage and Sweetgrass mingled with the smell of melted chocolate left too close to the heater, fragrances the air in sickening waves of sweet and medicinal plumes – And I knew ... in the fading light.

I feel the air has shifted. I hear a coyote crying. It wasn't yelping or howling, it was crying. I stare out into the backyard and see the yellow defeated grass, the moss invading the trees, the fresh cold rain falling in gentle brush strokes landscaping the winter. And I am afraid. And I knew.

"He die!" came her broken English trying to chronicle through her sobs across ten miles of phone lines and towers and a silent receiver, heavy breathing the only sound she hears. "He die!" she emphatically declares and I hate it, hate her for expecting me to know what to do or say. Tears begin to form in my eyes and I hate myself for not knowing what to say.

The coyote begins to cry

louder ... faster ... louder ... He and I used to fall asleep in each other's arms with the window open and the sound and smell of the rain filling the blackness of the night. I fit into the crook of his arm like a puzzle piece, long lost and found, gently taped together and brushed with a sealant guaranteed not to fall apart ... a complete puzzle of a little girl lost who happened upon shelter in a thunderstorm.

Silence crawls and has me on my knees

I do not want to feel this, breathless, unsure, afraid like a baby when she takes her first steps and knows she will fall. She also knows she has to get up again. And again. And again.

And again

Five years later, I can still smell the scent of melted chocolate and Sweetgrass and hear the sound of a coyote crying, comforting my loss, calling into the night, when you happen into my mind

a lone echo

melted chocolate

Sweetgrass

and a

a coyote crying

All this romance
is just Zanzibar.

What matters is a note
stuck by a magnetic carrot
to the refrigerator saying
Don't look for me I am gone.

~ ROBERT KELLY

An Epigraph for Zanzibar

(The rest of the letter that fell under the refrigerator,
written on pink Post-it notes in tiny, neat
handwriting with, surprisingly, no mistakes)

Please Don't look for me:
I have gone to Zanzibar.
I've gone to pet baby monkeys
and I've taken the car.

It feels like I'm choking on
cold cream of gruel
lumpy, bumpy, cold, and cruel
laying half-dead in your pool.

I've gone to feel the sand on my feet
and to write poems between the sheets –
something I have never done before –
and dance naked in the streets.

Perhaps I'll visit a sultan's palace
and eat exotic foods –
mango curry, coconut pilau;
and perhaps I'll take some nudes.

I'll send you a postcard,
perhaps a pic or two.
Don't forget to feed the dog
and let him out to poo.

Love, Irene

A Thousand Pictures

A poem paints a thousand pictures
naked to each human's soul
destined to reach us and take
our designer blinders off –
leaving us fully clothed
in a room full of naked strangers
while tears stream our faces
while we wonder why

They don't get it
why we can't figure it out.

I am an Indigenous woman
with brown skin
a brown mind
no beaded earrings for me
thank you very much –
a reminder of how a single bead
caused competitiveness among
the other brown minds now seeing
the possibilities of being better than
in pinks, golds, blues, purples, blacks, and – REDS.

I am a First Nations woman
with brown skin
a brown mind
that can laugh off abuse
and make a joke out of it
about how sexually experienced
I am because I have had years of
experience as a child
in a foster home
being protected from
my mother's alcoholism.

I am a First Nations Woman
with brown skin
a brown mind
who lost her mother
to alcohol –

I do not blame her for dying –
I do not blame her for giving up –
I don't blame her for not
praying hard enough –
or dreaming hard enough –

I'm not going to spend another twenty
years crying and blaming her for things –
beyond her control and I'm not going to cry
because she left me and my children too soon –

I am going to rejoice that she is no longer running
from the pain to the path of anywhere, everywhere
Just not here.

I am a First Nations Woman
with brown skin
a brown mind
brown thoughts
standing in my brown truth
I will paint a thousand pictures
with words slapping someone in the face
and rubbing others on the back
and planting brown seeds in other minds ...

Ancestors –

I can't imagine how painful
it was to watch people dying
all around you by a power
that wasn't even real in spirit –
nothing you could touch
like a newborn's downy hair –
but in another realm, held
the threat of death.

Ancestors –
Death answered many prayers
regardless of if you followed policy
procedure and just lay down
and gave up on the spot
and gave your children away
and found out God was never
a part of the planning.

Ancestors –
I hear your heart beat with
every youth that opens
their hearts to their culture
who opens their eyes just a bit more –
willing to learn, to accept,
and to change and mould
this power.

Ancestors –
Watching the souls being
killed off in a game of greed
and no matter what you did
it seemed to be a losing game –
and yet you continued forward.

Ancestors –
Thank you for not giving up
and not giving up the pieces
to the puzzle so that others
may one day stumble –
upon a piece of the puzzle
and stumble upon home
with the grace of an angry buffalo –
and perhaps even one day stay
and not be ashamed to partake
in ceremony, in healing prayer
and in letting ego live outside of self
walking as close to Mother Earth
as possible, feeling connection to her
and to us, one day they will be Ancestors too –

Ancestors –
You were never without a mother
never without a father
never without the answers
but you needed time to learn a new way,
a new way of thinking –
things were changing,
our children were being taken –
our women being hurt –
our men being broken –

Ancestors
I walk forward and write
and walk softly
In honour of you.

Best IntentiOns BrOken PrOMises

(Children in care, inspired by another mother so much like my own, who was not able to stop the memory demons from affecting her children)

MOMMY please dOn't tell Me
i aM cOMing hOMe
if there is even a sMall chance
that i aM nOt
please dOn't plant seeds in MY head
that aren't gOing tO grOw
please dOn't tell Me we will
MOve tO the cOuntrY and have a dOg
when YOu can't take care Of Me
please just tell Me YOu lOve Me
and that YOu will alwaYs lOve Me
but that YOu cannOt take care Of Me.
please explain tO Me that it is nOt MY fault
and that i aM the best thing tO happen tO YOur life
please dOn't plant seeds Of hOpe in MY head
that we will be tOgether again
sOMewhere far awaY in a better place
because MOM i lOve YOu tOO and can see
that YOu aren't able tO take care Of Me.
as Much as it hurts i knOw the creatOr
hOlds Me in his hands
and i ask creatOr tO hOld YOu tOO
because MOM i knOw YOu lOve Me
and i lOve YOu tOO
but YOu can't take care Of Me.
i knOw hOw Much YOu lOve Me
and I knOw there are reasOns whY YOu cannOt
take care Of Me and MOMMY
i dO nOt blaMe YOu but please dOn't
plant seeds Of hOpe in MY head
that One daY we will live bY the Ocean

help Me staY in realitY
bY just telling Me the truth
because i knOw sOMething is wrOng,
please just let Me knOw it isn't MY fault
and that i was the best thing tO happen tO YOu.
please respect MY lOve fOr YOu
bY nOt telling Me we will be tOgether again
even if there is OnlY a sMall chance i MaY nOt.
all i need tO knOw is hOw Much YOu lOve Me
and that it isn't MY fault
and that YOu will trY YOur best tO take care
Of YOurself sO that i can see YOu and
nOt crY at night waiting fOr YOu
tO take Me awaY tO anOther place
fOr OnlY MOthers and daughters
where there are nO trOubles
and nO sOcial wOrkers ...
just tell Me YOu lOve Me
and that it is nOt MY fault

that is all I need

tO all the children Of residential schOOls ...

(Inspired by Mechelle Pierre)

i hOpe YOur life is filled with lOve
frOM here On earth and frOM abOve.
i hOpe YOu can OvercOMe YOur fears
thrOugh faMilY, friends, and ManY healing tears.
i hOpe YOu can find YOur waY back hOMe
where YOu feel MOst safe, anYwhere YOu chOOse
just as lOng as YOu can be YOurself
tO laugh withOut shaMe and let gO Of pain.
i hOpe YOu can see the creatOr's plan fOr YOu
because YOu're still here and learning tO lOve
and sharing YOur knOwledge can bring abOut change
and a chance tO set things right in YOur heart.
i hOpe YOu sMile at the little things and pause
and reflect On hOw Much tiMe was needed tO bring it fOrth
because even a flOwer had tO be planted in Manure
tO blOssOM intO a resilient flOwer whO One daY will reunite
with the earth, but until then share the beautY and wealth Of healing
which is a cOntinuOus cYcle just like the earth and all her creatures.
bring fOrth new sMiles, new lOves, and new lives and reinvent Old waYs
tO give a child the will and strength tO push fOrth intO new territOrY
where it dOesn't hurt tO be a child and it dOesn't hurt tO laugh
and there's nO shaMe in being happY and there's nO waY tO break their hearts

and it's Ok tO be prOud because YOu have taught theM hOw special theY
are tO YOu and tO the creatOr ...

i hOpe YOu knOw just hOw strOng YOu are,
just hOw resilient,
just hOw beautiful,
just hOw knOwledgeable,
just hOw aMazing YOu are tO push fOrth

YOur wings tO flY again,
tO see beautY in the ugliness
because withOut the pain Of YesterdaY,
YOu wOuldn't be whO YOu are tOdaY ...
a teacher, a survivOr, a lOver Of life,
and the keeper Of stOries Of awful daYs
gOne bY ...

Walk a Mile in My Moccasins

Walk a mile in my moccasins

after the dust settles

and all that's left

are regrets, should-haves,

half "sorrys," and sad stories

Walk a mile in my moccasins

as I pretend to know how to parent

faking it and praying not to break it

into a million of I don't knows

and don't know how to forgive myself

and it was never taught

and the colour of forgiveness isn't brown –

Walk a mile in my moccasins

as I try to hold down a job to

put food on the particleboard table,

courtesy of Sally Ann –

Raise some children?

AND? Take care of myself?

And must pretend I know what to do

all the while holding my head

and heart crying, trying not to throw up

waiting for answers and reprieve

from a fixed deck of cards with no faces –

But I did watch TV –

Walk a mile in my moccasins

as the racism courses through

others' veins, blue-blooded chains

who write books on parenting

and self-help wherewithal, be-all-end-all

shoving it down my throat while

holding my neck between righteous hands,

who have never been abandoned,

shamed, blamed, or culturally raped

in another language you are now

just beginning to understand

Walk a mile in my moccasins,

as I bear the burden and pain

of our Ancestors who placed

so much hope in us and I am afraid

to fail and get swallowed up by time

and lack of disclosure and white papers

and wasted words falling upon closed ears

Walk a mile in my moccasins

as I try to put two and two

together again and still come

up with the letter 3 every time

cause I never understood why

the people in foster homes were

cruel to scrawny brown kids

Walk a mile in my moccasins

as I cry for a Mother

who never knew how to live,

who never knew how to love,

but she was oh so good at dying

Walk a mile in moccasins

as I look in the mirror

and see all the lost dreams

of the Ancestors who laid

down their lives at the cost

of their generations

so the future brown kids

could stand a chance

Walk a mile in my moccasins

as I shed daily tears

for all the lost brown women

who were once little brown girls

and hopefully at least once

basked in the sun without

a care in the world

beside their mother

with their tummies full

without a mournful tear

to shed, just yet.

Walk with me in my moccasins

as I pray daily for all

the brown men who learned

to suppress emotion and harness anger

who were once little brown boys

and hopefully at least once got to fish

with their brown dads in the mid-morning sun

with dried pemmican by their sides and smiles frozen

in that brown moment

Walk with me in my moccasins

as I try to tell the story

without hatred and self-pity

of a Creator who has always

walked with us when brown

was the wrong colour

and still is, almost everywhere.

Walk with me in my moccasins

and I'll tell you a story

of many a time when I wanted to be

walking with you in white shoes …

MOMMY i wOuld have

i wOuld have lOOked all

Over the wOrld

just tO find YOu

and i wOuld have

fOund YOu

i wOuld have held YOur hand and taught YOu hOw tO skip

and taught YOu tO sing and tO lOve what YOu hear

i wOuld have taught YOu tO saY nO, nO, nO, and nO

and hOw tO run and hOw tO tell,

and i wOuld alwaYs believe YOu and tell YOu sO.

i wOuld Make sure YOu were never hungrY

we'd gO fishing and snaring rabbits and have

a garden and fill it with lOts and lOts Of spinach

because it's YOur favOurite.

we'd watch the clOuds that pass us bY and cOunt

the daYs until YOu'd be Old enOugh tO gO tO schOOl

and i'd take YOu everY MOrning

and let YOu pick whatever YOu wanted tO wear

even if it was cOwbOY bOOts and shOrts

and purple tights

and if YOu never wanted

tO wear a dress again

i'd understand

i'd understand, i'd understand …

i wOuld have gentlY washed YOur bOdY

and tOld YOu abOut the wOnders and sanctities

Of a wOMan's bOdY and tOld YOu that we wOMen

were given a gift sO pOwerful and sacred

and tOld YOu abOut lOve and relatiOnships

and Making lOve and the difference

and I wOuld tell YOu tO lOve YOur bOdY

and that YOur bOdY was YOurs alOne

i wOuld have carried

YOu – just YOu

upOn MY

shOulders

On MY back

in MY arMs

fOr as lOng

and as far

as YOu needed Me tO

i wOuld have tOld YOu

i lOved YOu everY

MOrning and

everY night

after i tOld YOu

stOries i had weaved

Out Of watching YOu

survive and finish cOllege.

i wOuld have washed

YOur hair with

hOneY, leMOn,

and cedar water.

and brushed it

as YOu tOld Me

stOries YOu weaved

frOM YOur threads

Of pain and cOnfusiOn

and i wOuld have

brushed and brushed

and brushed YOur hair

and wOven it

with butterflY clips

behind YOur ears

Over and Over

and tOld YOu

the little girl in

YOur MeMOries

was a herO

with angel's, wings

with the gift

tO teach

Other little girls

hOw tO saY nO

and hOw tO run –

i wOuld have held

YOu tight upOn

MY lap

when YOu cried –

i wOuld have listened

and listened and listened

and listened sOMe MOre –

and been cOMfOrtable

in YOur silence

until YOu were readY

tO share YOur pain

i wOuld have held YOur head

clOse tO MY heart

sO YOu wOuld hear

MY heart's sOft sOng

and let it sOOthe YOu

like a babY

in MY wOMb –

i wOuld have dried

YOur cheeks

YOur eYes

with the sOftest

deerskin

i Made just fOr YOu.

i wOuld have Made

YOu a jingle dress

Out Of the sOftest, perfect buckskin

with twice the aMOunt Of snuff can lids

sO everYOne cOuld hear YOu as YOu danced

tO the beat Of YOur Own heart and vOice

sO everYOne cOuld hear YOu

becOMe One with MOther earth

i wOuld have put theM in jail

with MY bare hands

and MY entire being

if that was the OnlY justice

that cOuld be served.

just tO save YOu frOM

Years Of helpless anger

and taught YOu abOut the bad Men

and Of the unsearchable

answers YOu seeMed tO accept

theM as ...

then YOu and i wOuld have jOurneYed

tO the Ocean tO bathe tOgether

while the cOld, saltY water

washed their sins awaY

and until YOu tOld Me it was Over

and tiMe tO stand On Our feet again.

i wOuld have walked

and walked and walked

thrOugh all YOur

Mistakes

chOices

and paths

Yet nOt taken

Mind in Mind

heart in heart

hand in hand

 i wOuld have knelt dOwn

 lOOked intO YOur eYes

and apOlOgized

Over and Over

fOr huManitY and

fOr nOt being there

when YOu needed theM

and begged YOu tO reach

beYOnd Others Mistakes

tO see with the eYes Of YOur sOul

the pOwer Of absOlute truth

and tO lOOk beYOnd YOurself

fOr the fault Of Others ...

and give theM back their burden

that was never yOurs tO begin with

i wOuld have tOld YOu that YOu were

a gift frOM the creatOr –

i wOuld have tOld YOu that

peOple whO hurt the creatOr's children

wOuld never have peace

when death

called and that theY

wOuld never have tiMe

tO earn the fOrgiveness

befOre theY tOOk their

last guiltY breaths

and that theY'd

relive all the sOrrOw

and reap the fear theY sOwed –

then i wOuld have held YOu tight

and tOld YOu hOw beautiful

YOu are when YOu sMile

and when YOu crY

and hOw Much jOY and

new hOpe YOu bring tO MY life

i wOuld have tOld YOu YOur tears

were Made Of mountain water and

Meant YOu were alive and willing tO fight

fOr YOur right tO see YOur face

YOur eYes

YOur spirit

In everY bOdY Of water

everYwhere we'd gO

we'd staY near the water

and see what

YOu alwaYs wanted tO see –

i wOuld have let YOu crY in MY arMs

rested upOn MY chest

and strOked YOur head

and guided YOur hair tO the sOft

fOld behind YOur ear

i wOuld have kissed YOur

brOwn beautiful saltY swOllen eYes

and let the tears clean YOur sOul

i wOuld have sat there and taught YOu

hOw tO crY

and the beautY in it

and the difference between

lOve and hate, and YOur rights

and nOt be afraid tO vOice thOse rights.

i wOuld have cried with YOu

i wOuld have had YOu teach Me

hOw tO crY and how to be angrY

and we wOuld have pOunded rOcks

tOgether in an eMptY fOrest

tO hear the angrY cYclOnes of sOund

reverberate back

Making us feel real

if that's what YOu

wanted tO dO –

Or we cOuld have just

ran and ran and ran

until Our sOuls caught up.

i lOve YOu,

i wOuld saY

and wait fOr YOu

tO be cOmfortable tO saY it.

i wOuld saY i'M sOrrY

fOr hu-man-itY –

just dON't

dON't build NO gOd-fearing church

ON my sliver Of barreN laNd

dON't build nO "iNdiaNs ONly" schOOls

dON't shOw me darwiNism first-haNd

NOr teach me abOut hatred

dON't take my mOther's tONgue

aNd sileNce her fOrever

dON't make me sigN white papers

after yOu've chaNged my Name

dON't take my blOOd aNd spill it

dON't take my childreN's sOuls

aNd tOss them iN the media fire

dON't take away my buffalO

NOr my deer aNd rabbits

dON't give me scratchy blaNkets

filled with small pOx aNd shame

fOr NOt kNOwing hOw to heal myself

frOm New diseases i've Never seen befOre

dON't make me driNk pOlluted water

and say yOu're NOt tO blame

dON't watch my peOple get sick

aNd seNd us bOdY bags

aNd say it was aN accideNt

The Star Treks

The stars gaze and examine me from the dark backdrop of the sky.

Finally – one cloudless night I see just how brown am I.

Venus looks intently, deep down into my soul – and I am lost,

Even quite barren, over the power lines and matrilineal pillage.

Orion aligns straight and tall through the gateway of it all –

And I am helpless to fix and mourn the dead stars that fall

And I swear last night, by my own accord, I saw it all

Or maybe it was just a wish to be and see further truth

And maybe get away from it all and man's deadened roots.

For I put myself on hold just to gaze up into the backdrop

That silences the night and makes one wonder and ponder

The questions unanswered by day and one moment

In the night – do I fear my very own plight staring at something

That is bigger and more abstract than I could ever know

And truly understand Mother Earth's need to change and to grow?

I promised the dying stars that flickered the second before death

Who blinked for me and shut their eyes a second too late,

That I would fight for what is right and good and for what I should.

But I just see the opposite of what the night sees and holds

And something isn't right as I stare and examine earth's body crumbling

Just how far will I go to obtain the weary truths of the past?

Of a long time ago when life wasn't ruled by hands of time,

Nor faces of desperation cutting through spiritual falsehoods.

And forget the deadlines and the daily ritual acceptance of

Traffic jams; even the jams in my mind – so I don't question my sanity?

Or question anyone else's or ask if it is all real or maybe it's just a dream

Concocted from the recesses of another's crippling fears?

But as I stare and ponder life and the millions of things

Through life's edges and precipices and broken rings

That threaten the circle into submission that no one claims to see

As the seconds, minutes, hours, days pass and no one's ever free.

Their sanity, my sanity, all our sanities, or is it just only me

Who sees the stars brightly shining and blinking for all to see?

It is too busy for me said the Man in the Moon and I will not come out

For I may waste whatever light I provide, proliferate and burn out

Between the cities' orbs of light and man's fight to have it all

Or die trying like the very star I saw last night flicker and die

Before my very eyes, with one last twinkling shudder

As I realize – just how small am I. Just how small am I.

Gazing into the backdrop of the sky

As I watch the stars slowly submit and die ...

1998 (DAD)

he hAD three DAys to live.

hAnging on for reDemption.

but i DiDn't know thAt.

wAsn't supposeD to know thAt.

i clung to DAD.

helD onto whAt wAs left.

cAncer riDDen.

feAr in his eyes.

knowing he was Dying

AnD not being Able to right

the pAst AnD this he knew –

i knew i woulDn't.

be Able to fix it.

time An enemy –

history mADe sure of thAt.

mADe sure

i wAs uncomfortAble.

cAlling you DADDy.

never wAs close enough.

to smell his AftershAve.

     like All the other kiDs.

          who remembereD their DADs –

               not even sure if you even wore

or coulD AfforD AftershAve.

                         but you DiD smell like smoke.

AnD i knew you Drank coffee.

     he left me when i wAs A kiD

          with my religious grAnDmother.

                         whose feet were plAnted in two worlDs.

one nAture, the other cAtholic chAins.

     prAying for reDemption with sweetgrAss

          surrounDing the rosAry.

                         i knew how to prAy to jesus.

AnD how to hAte him.

     behinD closeD Doors.

          AnD offer sweetgrAss.

               to jesus As he sAt in the curio.

                    i took communion.

                         jesus tAsteD like bAnnock.

without mArgArine …

An "Indian" Never Dies Peacefully

Colonization Teaches Hate.

I hated myself because of it, it mystifies me, lies to me, confuses me, and always brings me to my knees; it tears me to little pieces that scatter in the lone wind, landing in different parts of the world I've never been and could never dream to go to, after all I was at the very end of the world, on a small reserve that ended by the lake. Reading brought me to Africa where the lions, giraffes, rhinos, and elephants roamed the land and hungry children thought about being me, with plenty of food, while I thought of them having plenty of love, and wondered which was worse? Was Maslow's Hierarchy of Needs wrong in stating food comes before love?

I read *National Geographic* at school once and the spread, with graphic pictures, was of a mother who watched her child starving. The love and sorrow written on her face was undeniable and I wished someone loved me that much too. I wished I could read the love for me upon someone's face and then I'd know I could make it instead of just faking my life to pretend my family wasn't just surviving. Here I had enough food but not enough love, there they had no food but plenty of love; which was worse? I fantasized about being a child in Africa with plenty of love, nothing to eat but at least I had a mother who cried for the state I was in and who stroked my head lovingly and I was always in her thoughts. My imagination, love of reading, and a few TV shows took me all over the world, out of my life and into fresh starts onto clean pages in my head that I rewrote each and every day. My conclusion later in life was my mother knew how to love, she didn't know how to stay; too many memory demons of abuse chased her, and she could only hide behind the shroud of alcohol and violent relationships that in her mind resembled the closest thing to love she ever knew.

We managed to get one channel with tin foil and rabbit ears and we would watch shows like *The Beachcombers*, *Coronation Street*, and *Sesame Street*. Around holidays like Christmas there were specials airing over the remote airwaves like *Rudolph the Red-Nosed Reindeer* or movies that touched me where no one else was able to. Santa was always nice to children and Rudolph found himself after being mistreated and shunned. I was going to find those places where children were treated nice and little girls found themselves. I left home at fourteen, eager to leave a barren land with no hope and possibly find some in another land way past the lake filled with leeches, outside of the reservation; about as foreign as you can get especially when as a child you think you are already at the end of the world, getting ready to drop off at any time. "Anything would be better than here," I thought even at six years old, always dreaming of one day leaving, never coming back, and finding my mom who let the demons chase her to places where people acted like lions.

I had my first thought of suicide when I was nine years old while washing my face. The fake, sad yellow of the bathroom surrounded me casting a lonely glow I felt deep in my heart and I knew what it was like to truly be alone. My saddened reflection already knew too much and I didn't want to be here getting ready to walk to church for another round of how God is good and how Jesus would save me. I didn't want to learn about a God who didn't care about me when I was being sexually and physically abused. I remember thinking that God did not exist or if he did, he didn't want to help me and I hated him. I hated him for my mother and father leaving me, I hated him for allowing abuses to happen, and I hated him for allowing me to be born "Indian." I thought that possibly he didn't help brown people, after all Jesus in church had blue eyes, brown hair, and pale skin. Any chance I could, I swore at him. How could a God exist and allow me to be sexually abused and beaten for telling? How could he take my father and mother away from me? How could he leave me in this horrible place if I was his child? I guess it takes more than this to give up and try to find a way to die with dignity and to be remembered as something other than just another "Indian" who until recently nobody heard of or read about. It's all stats without names or faces or even headstones to mark that they have ever been here, no one's problem anymore. Headstoneless.

My Uncle Jimmy committed suicide on a calm rainy day when the drops of rain felt warm and soothing, in the middle of summer when I was nine. My mother fell to the floor when the cop told her "Is Jimmy your brother? Well he hung himself and died." The cop didn't even wait for her answer to claim her brother Jimmy. I remember Mom, and it could have even been your mom, continuously stamping her feet on the grey, peeling linoleum and she couldn't stop crying. Her thinning hair matted to her face and her eyes swelled before my eyes. I can still hear the grass dancing in the wind through the open window and feel the slight coolness of the breeze that entered our dark basement suite. He had hung himself with a belt in a white closet from a solid wood dowel. I remember those dowels and how thick and strong things were made in the old days, I know because I would hang from the same dowel Jimmy would eventually see as a solution to his pain and sadness. The eggshell-white paint hadn't even had time to gather a brownish yellow hue from all the smoking that he was supposed to do in his lifetime. He was in his thirties. I never really knew him, he was always in jail or off in another city drinking and using drugs and I hated him for it. He was nothing like the uncles I saw on TV. As I grew older, I wondered just what pushed him over the edge to imagine an eggshell-white closet as a final resting place without saying goodbye to anyone and leaving my mom to question whether she could have saved him had she been there. And me questioning if she had saved him, what would he have been doing and would he have tried again in a different closet or maybe even in jail. Maybe, just maybe, he would have become a stone pillar for all the family to be drawn to when they were weary? Or would he have been amid the fentanyl crisis. As an "Indian," it doesn't take much after years and years of mistreatment, objectification, and suppression, to give in to spur-of-the-moment suicides without goodbyes. Time seems to calm lives down, but sometimes time moves too slowly to give any hope and answers. Answers are like stars, out of reach and dying everyday moment by moment, and aren't really tangible to us as beings because we can't touch them, but night after night they come out, and when we aren't absorbed by trauma, can we ever really notice them and give them the space for more thoughts besides the past?

My Aunt Donna was only eighteen with her first child when she put a shotgun in her mouth and pulled the trigger. I was about ten and I can still see her smiling face as she played with her son perched on her tummy, making the baby giggle uncontrollably and it made me jealous. I wanted to laugh uncontrollably too. I wanted to be that baby who was able to laugh and not feel guilty for being happy. Donna and the baby were so happy on my mother's orange and brown crocheted bedspread, with the rain gently falling from the sky and tapping softly on the window. Rain always knocking as a foreshadowing of deaths to come. The crocheted bedspread I remember so well, Mom must have crocheted it when she thought she may actually have a chance at happiness, and possibly for once the memory demons would quit chasing and death would stop catching up to her thoughts. My mom used to say, "Don't laugh too much, or bad things will happen." I thought about this years later and my only explanation is she must have felt that if you kept your emotions even and downplayed your happiness, then sadness and sorrow wouldn't feel as horrible, that maybe if you kept yourself in the pits of sorrow, nothing could ever devastate you again.

My Uncle Leonard also used a gun to escape the memory demons of his past. One day he pointed it at his head and pulled the trigger like it was the most normal thing in the world to do. And for him, maybe it was. He was in his twenties. Some his age were collecting diplomas, medals, and grad gifts; he was collecting bullets, prayers, and playing "Indian" roulette with a cocked shotgun. At the time, in my child brain, it was normal for "Indians" to have family members commit suicide. Funerals were normal and there were always sweet cakes.

My Auntie Mary died from cirrhosis of the liver and that's the way she wanted it. My mother begged her to quit drinking once, just after the doctor told her she was definitely going to die if she didn't quit immediately. My aunt told us that she was going to leave this world drinking and that it was the only way she was ever happy and could forget and to just bloody well leave her alone. Even though she was bleeding from all her orifices, she drank herself to death and was buried on a rainy Vancouver day without a headstone. "Indians" don't want headstones, they cost too much money and maybe if you expected a headstone and didn't get one, maybe just maybe it meant you were right and that you were never good enough. Maybe that's why they all want to be cremated and scattered in lone winds across dreams and landscapes where pain didn't exist anymore. It's only the loved ones who want them but can't afford them. What kind of "Indian" finances a headstone and gets denied because of a unpaid phone bill? The kind of "Indian" that loves their family and still can't afford a headstone. Better tack that onto the list of whys of why I'm still not good enough. My mom wanted one for her sister and I guess her sister gave her specific instructions that they not spend money on a headstone. Auntie Mary knew my mom could never afford one unless she paid in tears and ground stones.

My Uncle Jerry's death is a mystery. My mother believed wholeheartedly that it was the police who killed him. She said the last time anyone ever saw him was the day before he died, in the back of a police car. Jerry was found in an industrial area, outside of the city in the winter, beaten up with no shoes, no socks, and no jacket. She said that when she went to identify the body, his feet, face, and hands were frostbitten. I didn't believe her when she said someone did this to him and it may have been the police. Many years later I read *Starlight Tour* by Susanne Reber and Robert Renaud, and finally believed her, but what can anybody do about it twenty or so years later? What can you do about it but mourn when you have no money, no voice, and no hope, and you're an "Indian" hoping to die peacefully?

One of my cousins hung himself from the rafters of an unfinished ceiling. He was discovered by another cousin, his brother who I'm sure is still haunted by this event. We were both in our late twenties or early thirties when he decided that he didn't want to be in this world of heartache and pain, with no answers forthcoming. His heart and soul must have had enough and time didn't pass quickly enough to offer up a solution for him to grasp onto. Days on the reservation pass so slowly and it's worse when you have no hope. We played together as children and boy could he ever hit the baseball far out into Uncle's field. He must have felt so proud on those days when he would be chosen first to play on a team. A team of "Indian" kids wanting to play and hit the ball far past where the bullshit grew – a moment to be normal, a moment to shine when hell was always around the corner and even sleep brought minimal relief because you never knew when you would get woken up, or when the next death would be.

My Uncle Clarence died from addiction and disease. I cut him down once from a shower dowel in the bathroom during a suicide attempt. I was sixteen and all my mom could do was stand there and scream and watch her baby brother hang there like a suit of clothes. It's probably the only thing I could do if I had seen my brother hanging by the throat from a shower pole with a white sheet wrapped around his neck, turning blue, eyes and lips swollen almost twice the size. Years later, I question why he wasn't helped sooner; the ambulance attendants left him at his home, making him promise he wouldn't do it again and take up their time. They all had a good laugh about it on the green grass where dandelions grew like wildfire, my mom went to her AA meeting and my uncle went uptown to drink. Just another crisis averted, and things went back to a different kind of normal for different kinds of folks.

Frank Paul died of hypothermia after being released from custody at 8:30 p.m. He was left in an alley by a police officer. What is it like to know that no one cares and that they can leave you in an alley not caring whether you died or not? What was it like to be the officer who left a human being in an alley in the cold dead of night with snowflakes swirling all around like an old Christmas movie you see on TV every year? What is it like to know that you were responsible for another human being's death? How many excuses ran through his mind, like "I thought for sure the cold would wake him up; it's not my fault he had nowhere to go and the jails were full; it's his own fault for choosing his lifestyle; he would have died sooner rather than later"; or maybe, just maybe, he could put it out of his mind like yesterday's paid bill and never think of it again, not seeing himself as half the problem. Frank Paul was someone's child, someone's sibling, someone's friend, and he could have been a father. I think he finally found peace when he took his last breath and his soul finally said goodbye in the twirling snow with the lights dancing, and he didn't feel the cold of the night or the cold of humanity anymore.

I remember as a child adults asking each other if they saw "so-and-so" and when the last time was and still not file a report: as if it was normal for an "Indian" to go missing and deep within their "Indian hearts" they knew no one would care except the family who could do nothing about it anyway but wonder and ask where "so-and-so" was and perhaps wonder if they would ever see them again.

The "Starlight Tours" of Saskatoon haunt me because at the time all the "Indians" knew this could potentially happen and was happening and still were powerless to do anything about it but be afraid and cautious, not even sure if travelling in pairs was a deterrent but maybe it was if you had a Caucasian friend with you, who knows. Rodney Naistus, Lawrence Wegner, Neil Stonechild, just to name a few "Indian" men who passed away in the dead cold of night dreaming of being in a warm bed and wondering why being "Indian" had to hurt. Imagine for a second the fear they felt and how alone in the middle of nowhere they were with no chance of somebody passing by but perhaps only another cop car. Somebody loved these men, they were someone's children, someone's brother, uncle, perhaps even father. They had hopes and dreams too but not the normal kind you see in books and movies. It costs too much to dream as an "Indian" because you were reaching for the stars and every "Indian" knows you can never touch the stars. Besides, stars die anyway. One minute they are way up there in the sky and the next minute they are gone ... poof ... Apparently the stars we see in the sky died a long time ago and we are only registering the information now, just like "Indians." Some of us died a long time ago. Perhaps they always meant to go home, perhaps they dreamed about a good meal and seeing a loved one, just perhaps they wanted to for once be normal and go to school and be treated with dignity; maybe dignity is a dream to those who aren't allowed to have them because the intangible colonialism disease decided so by some fluke, knowing it could not pillage this earth if the "Indian" was between Mother Earth and its ideas, which always come to fruition by the sheer fact that the ego is alive and well today.

I remember not hearing from my brown mother for spans of time, the longest was two years, and all I could do was wonder when she was coming back or I thought perhaps she died trying to come back. One day she does come back but what if she doesn't the next time? There would be nothing this brown little "Indian" girl could do except miss her mother and pray for her safe return and scream and swear at god for allowing this shit to go on. My mother could have been on that list of Missing and Murdered Indigenous Women and Girls. I could have been on that list and one day maybe one of my daughters, maybe one of my granddaughters. Objectified as if we came with the land and could be pillaged and tossed aside like dead trees in the forest in the way of a shiny white waterfront property made of dead trees. According to the RCMP's National Operational Overview, "police-recorded incidents of Aboriginal female homicides and unresolved missing Aboriginal females ... total 1,181 – 164 missing and 1,017 homicide victims." In my heart and soul, I know that there are more missing women then 1,181; those numbers are just the reported loved ones missing. What about all the unreported cases? These women were mothers, daughters, sisters, aunts, wives, partners, friends, writers, artists, dreamers, baseball players, music lovers who were objectified and treated like less than human beings because of the colour of their skin. Being brown, with a big helping of colonization: a true recipe for disaster. Colonization is such a broad term and I use it in its broadest sense to include the four thousand (at least) deaths at residential schools between 1870 and 1996. These are only reported numbers, it's the unreported numbers that remain a secret within someone's soul and destroyed records that they have taken, or perhaps will take, to the grave. Maybe they will die without peace just like an "Indian" who never truly knew how to live but who knew how to die.

It was through education, counselling, and plenty of tears that I was finally able to understand why "Indians" never die peacefully. Colonization is a disease that attacks you from the inside and tries to attach itself to your bones so your future generations feel it and never forget who's "boss." It makes its ideas your own and makes you feel like a failure for never fitting in anywhere. It steals your identity and in its place leaves plenty of masks that you must choose from to put on before every unstaged play that you trudge through faking your entire being because you never learned how to be happy. It sings you songs you never heard before and don't want to listen to but in order to survive, you must. It tells you who you are and where you must go in the face of racism and adversity. It puts you to bed at night humming a nuclear lullaby that surely you must not pass on to your children but do so anyway unconsciously (ripple effect). It is a silent disease many suffer in silence, until they can bear no more. That is when they stop playing the game, stop putting on different masks, stop believing in goodness, stop hoping, stop trying to catch up to the unknown; instead they turn to alcohol and drugs to place a thin mask of numbness over the entire world and seal their fate and at least they were in control of something. They know that it is easier to make bad decisions than it is to make good ones especially because you know you'll have to fight everyday of your life to bring about a baby step of change, a drumbeat of heart that murmurs to our future great-grandchildren. Maybe in dying and giving up they gave hope to others who struggle to raise their children just the opposite of whatever road they saw their brothers, sisters, fathers, mothers travel, and maybe, just maybe, they were "Indian" Jesuses who sacrificed themselves for the good of the whole, to leave an example of roads painfully travelled and where the dead ends are. One thing I am sure of is that whatever pain and sorrow I have witnessed or felt first-hand, my children are better off than past generations and their children will be better off than their upbringing and maybe one day they will pick up the drum and sing a lullaby to their little ones because starting over and adapting and reintegrating is better than giving up and forgetting and better than masking the self with anything other than what you truly feel deep down inside. It's alive, the drummed heartbeat of mother and Mother Earth, the breath of life through pain and reaching the other side of the river of colonization and finally accepting the past and maybe, just maybe, writing about it for defense, healing, and understanding. They say when an Elder dies, more knowledge is lost, but maybe, just maybe, they will come to us in words, art, and resolution and send us an army of youth who will cry for the past, sing for the future, and make it right for the future "Indians" to come so we may one day be able to die peacefully...

I sit in a barely pink room

Surrounded by ashes and dust

Memories and rust

Feeling dead inside

Because they all tried

To beat death

At its own game

Opportunity did not knock

They chased it

With a passion

To surrender...

Untitled

I hear MY babY crYing

frOM acrOss the narrOw

hallwaY –

the Other half Of MY heart

calls tO Me.

white puckered cups

handed tO Me

frOM nasallY nurses

their fOOtprints

eMbedded in rOck

falling cOncrete slabs.

the heater hisses

nurses cackle

talking abOut

patients and lacking patience

and weight lOss.

anOther call bell rings

and the fOOtsteps sOund

in the hallwaY cluMp sigh

cluMp sigh cluMp sigh.

i hear MY babY calling

frOM acrOss the hallwaY

MY insides feel like

theY are falling Out.

cOld unearthlY flOOrs

whY dO YOu wear white

such a stark cOntrast from brOwn

YOu are sO far reMOved frOM us.

tiptOe sigh tiptOe sigh – i gO tO MY babY ...

BROTHER

(Sibling lOve when we were in foster care.
Inspired bY Vera Manuel's pOem "Brother.")

i miss yOu BROTHER.

THE yEaRs aRE shORT.

THE days aRE lOng.

i sTood on THE chaiR.

my BROTHER.

and waTcHEd yOu cRy.

as i TRiEd TO wasH disHEs.

wiTH seven-yEar-Old Hands.

i cOuld nOt undERsTand yOur TEaRs.

i undERsTOOd THE fEaR.

yOuR small hands.

fOuR fingERs in yOuR MOuTH.

TRying TO mufflE puppy sOunds.

yOuR THumb lEfT OuT.

By THE sidE Of yOuR small BERRy mOuTH.

yOuR pincHEd facE.

wET wiTH salT.

dRiEd snOT.

fROm yEsTERdaY.

yOuR haiR sTanding Tall.

fREshly cuT By sTRangERs.

nO mOTHER tO cOmB it.

THE smEll Of fREsh Rain.

puncHEs THE aiR.

shE puncHEs yOu.

THE ligHT HiTs THE TEal cupBOaRds.

THE ROOm dRaBBER.

THan it was inTEndEd TO BE.

BEcausE nO lOvE REsidEd THERE.

i sTOOd On THE cHaiR BROTHER.

washing disHEs.

THE spOOns TalkEd TO Each OTHER.

i made THEm.

THE plaTEs slEpT.

THE pOTs wERE nEw fRiEnds.

THE waTER a swimming pOOl.

i'm sOrry my BROTHER.

i jusT sTOOd On THE cHaiR.

and waTcHEd yOu cRy.

i miss yOu BROTHER.

Striking Things

St. Joseph's Hill in the winter –

Kokum's going-to-town dresses –

Bright flower patterns –

Precious head scarf –

Dentures in –

Proud and prim –

Off to town for her –

Monthly outing –

Ice cream on the list –

How now brown cow she would say –

The dog's hopeful eyes –

Wanting food, wanting love –

Petting the strays –

Showing them my empty hands –

Sliding down St. Joseph's –

Putting away groceries –

Bought from Kokum's pension –

St. Joseph's catholic pilgrimages –

Kokum's Sweetgrass-picking skills –

Berry-picking hands blood red –

Praying for mercy for her offspring –

Survival 50/50

DOGS

On the reservatiOn

there are tOO many DOGS

brOwn Ones

black Ones

brOwn and black Ones

jet black, glazeD Over

with Dirt and hOpe

Of GlitterinG sun

hittinG muD puDDle

a small shape

i take One hOme

the rest Die

withOut a name –

Mother Earth – the Cherry Blossom in Me

Mother Earth, cherry blossom
The cherry blossom in me ...
I want to regenerate every year with a force
so powerful that my winding roots are shaken,
and my core is conditioned to welcome rebirth –
that is the essence of spirit and is the only reality.

I want to be free, meditating in the gentle wind,
our life-giving flowers gently, slowly
falling in pink swirls round and round
landing with gentle retreat, waiting
for the seeds of bodily encompassment –
but this year I melt warily and solitarily
into the ground with new hopes of
the possibilities of new life springing forth –
virtuous and free and they will know it is me.
They will know it has always been me ...
Mother Earth and all my children ...
Pink precious flower, life-giver, soul redeemer
the cherry blossom in me and I will not
believe it is all over even for a second.
My soul will not allow me a moment to forget
that the cherry blossom in me is to raise indigo,
to raise a pure soul untouched by greed,
unharmed by falling away unjustified half-truths,
misjudgments and delicate trusting hearts so
devastated by the state of the world and suffering
for humans' ability to lower human spiritual condition.
The cherry blossom in me wants to gently
float in the wind atop a warm life breeze
and recreate new beautiful life into
a world with hatred littered as artificial sustenance
against the lost and chosen misled of the world ...
The cherry blossom in me ...

Mama's Moon

She used to smile at me, you know,
whenever we were alone.
It would extend past her grief,
past her history and shame:
not hers to bear – never was
and she never, ever knew that.

Her eyes would shine and twinkle,
just for me; her part-time daughter.
The past always one step ahead of her.
She said she never meant to leave,
never meant to plant roses without roots.

She would tell me secrets and dreams,
about the places she had been
and hadn't been afraid to go –
she said being a child was scarier
than sleeping under a bridge
on a snowfall starless night –
She said the snowy sky was so orange
with whirling, dancing snow spirits
so real, so pure, so close that she prayed
so she may somehow touch the sky
and feel the realness, the pureness,
and the closeness as she prayed
for her children she left behind.
She said she did not want the ghosts
of her past to capture her children
and draw them under the cloak of
addiction, abuse, and hopelessness,
and eventually an untimely death.
She said she never had a chance –

She said to be near her, to feel her,
I would only have to look at the moon
and just know that she would be thinking
of me and loving me from under the same moon.

She said that if I hugged myself
and thought of her, she would feel
my thoughts travelling the emotional
and physical distance and just be –
with me on her mind and in her heart
and she in mine – "for always," she would whisper.

She used to smile at me, you know,
whenever we were alone,
it would extend past her grief,
past her history and shame
not hers to bear – never was
and she never, ever knew that.

It has always been my Mama's moon.

I forget

About the little girl I once was
once was and still am and will continue to be
in the face of needless suffering,
crippling wars slaying spirituality
and I am threatened by my own silence;
leaving truth dead by the side of the road
drying in the sun soon to disappear
like the snow falling upon the rust-
stained polar bears tired and hungry
tired of being hungry ...

Our Mother is hurt and lying all alone
like an animal by the side of the road ...
I heard her sigh for the last time
when she succumbed to man-made destiny
that she saved the ice age for, but used too soon.

Her children are suffering under the constraints
of an impossible one-way cycle
that was never meant to be;
never meant to open Pandora's box
and pray to figure it out later.

Our children's children will suffer
and she knew this, we knew this
and they will know this
when once again history will be written
by one mind and read by twenty million and one
without even realizing just how
needless it really, really was
and just how much guilt and death
time can erase like the white
fine dust etched on chalkboards
that once stood tall and superior

over the spiritually oppressed ones
or so the man wrote for thousands
to read by candlelight
after a long day's repentant work
plugging in your cellphone
next to your head –
dreaming in pixels and technicolour

Tears of anger and hunger
trail tirelessly down her face,
which is my face and your face
and still we are helpless,
standing by the side of the road
with our heads down and no direction;
greed has shamed us,
and blackened our roots
for I too feel the power
that money can buy
if only for the shortest while
until I fall asleep just to do it
all over again tomorrow and
tomorrow's tomorrow –

I am saddened that I even know this
and even sadder that I too will
be left lying by the side of the road
if I do not close my mind from greed and see;
starvation of the spirit is imminent.

Once when I was nine
I asked my father if water
would ever run out
and he turned to me,
shook his head and said

"NO, of course not!
Where on earth did you ever get
an idea like that?"
He passed away in '98
at the age of fifty-one
still believing water
could never possibly run out.
I guess what he really meant
was not in his lifetime.
Once something becomes a commodity
it is destined to run out and become
a greedy man's lifeline.
I guess when your only toys are
books, paper, and No. 10 grey pencils
you could only see in black and white
wrong and right
but was still too little to fight
and still am while I cower in the corner
and see myself hugging my knees
close to my body, making myself
as invisible and as blameless as possible.

I sit on the floor among the clutter
and consumer righteousness
trying to become un-invisible
through my thoughts, mind, and my paper
and splash my feeble, useless fury
on recycled paper; another twenty trees
lie dying by the side of the road
just so I could have a paper voice
because when it comes right down to it
I still am the little girl cowering in the corner
with the paper voice.

I once thought I could change
the way ignorant people think
but once those designer blinders are on
no one wants to take them off
for fear of seeing what's directly
in front of our faces, our eyes – My hypersensitivity
to the pain and suffering of others.
I sometimes forget the little girl
who once questioned the abundance of water
instead I still question the sanity.
But this time I only ask how long…
and take a sip of water from a paper cup
and at least try to savour it.
Savour the water I bought and poured into a paper cup
upon which was written "Save the trees" –

Cross-Culture's Baby on the Way

Why do you speak only in the moment?
Covering the past with artifacts?
Keeping every vulnerable thought to yourself
Like Buddha unrealized at a casino
Watching all the blinking lights and they still mean nothing
You love absolutely no one – even yourself.
Where do you go at night?
All alone in your head.
And must I learn your ways?
Of being alone and beyond sight.
I imagine you loving freely
Without the chains of the past
And I am stricken with doubt.
I want our child to be your sustenance –

You have taught me humility
And walking in another's moccasins
And how to cry alone
And how to pretend I do not feel.

Why do you run?
Instead of walking a steady pace?
With love, belief, and grace
And believe tomorrow a yesterday
And today a tomorrow –

Two worlds melt into one – She is born September 27.

Stand   BY   The   Last   Stream

Mother,   I   can   hear   You   cry
with   every   pipeline   being
laid   to   unrest   deep   in   Your   folds,
deep   in   Your   layers.
I   can   hear   You   cry
and   those   who   believe
know   why   –

Stand   by   the   last   stream
it's   only   a   matter   of   time
and   stories   will   be   told
of   a   time   when   water   was
clean   and   .   free.
It   will   be   a   fairy   tale   in
mythical   books   sold   at
treasure   emporia.
It   will   be   what   dreams
are   made   of
and   what   man   will
die   for.

Stand   by   the   last   stream
watch   it   struggle
p   i   t   i   f   u   l   l   y   ,
trying   to   complete   the   circle
with   nothing   left   to   prove.

Stand   by   the   last   stream
gather   around   it
to   pray   hard   this   doesn't   end
the   intentions   of   Mother   Earth.
Remember   the   slow   trickles,
the   last   sounds   anyone   ever   hears
of   a   time   when   water   was   clear
and   a   time   when   it   was   free,

a   time   when   water   fell   from   the   sky
clear   droplets,   clear   droplets
that   could   be   tasted
as   they   fell.

Stand   by   the   last   stream
that   feeds   the   life   of   our   animals
who   trusted   Mother   Earth
to   always   provide.
Imagine   the   new   bear   or   the   new   child
not   knowing   where   the   last   stream   is.
What   will   become   of   them?

Stand   by   the   last   stream,
the   last   untouched   source
of   life,   peace,   and   renewal,
gurgling,   choking   for   breath
and   space
not   a   fish   in   sight
because   they   are   all   in   farms   and   zoos.

Stand   by   the   last   stream
as   our   children's   children
gather   round   and   wonder   why,
saying   they   could   have   done   a   better   job,
and   they'd   be   right.

Stand   by   the   last   stream,
with   your   friends   and   loved   ones
and   reminisce   about   a   time
when   you   could   reach   in   with   both   hands,
almost   in   prayer,   and   cup   the   water
and   drink   straight   from   Mother   Earth   –
the   breast   of   humankind.

Stand   by   the   last   stream
wondering   what   happened,
turning   into   a   third   world   country

as the trees that once stood tall,
fall by the wayside waiting to be
turned into more paper for more
signatures and stamps of approval
to go ahead and destroy the last stream.

Stand by the last stream
with your child looking on
at the last crystal clear water
trickling to an end
and try to find the , words
to explain.
Try and explain what no one
will understand and hindsight is

2 0 / 2 0 .

Stand by the last stream
as money floats by
instead of fish,
and gold can't be drunk,
and silver can't be eaten,
and diamonds can't keep you warm,
and animals can't be saved,
and technology can't pray for you,
and the trees rot on the ground oil,
and you can't give a newborn oil,
and not even the dandelions will grow,
and the birds won't call,
while children swarm singing
in empty fields
by the last stream,
and the pictures you see in your head
will only be a story
sold in treasure emporia
and the only thing left will be regret.

while standing by the last stream – – –

(Untitled until further notice)

Do you realize just how beautiful you are?

Just how much light comes from within?

Do you know you are a divine creation?

Made perfect to walk this earth in Creator's eyes?

You have always had a Mother and a Father

A Mother so resourceful she feeds and houses you –

Her resilience the reason you must go on

You have always had a Father

Who has always walked with you –

Step for step even when you fell.

You have always had family, those kinship ties

especially when you needed it most.

Just a glimmer or a whole star is shown to you.

Just when you need it most.

Do you know how precious you are?

Your spirit longs to be awakened.

Your wish to be free from the pangs of loneliness.

Your body wishes to be cared for

and your heart and soul want release.

Do you know you were meant to be? Mistakes and all?

You weren't meant to hide behind alcohol nightmares

or drug-induced temporary mirage of wellness

or obsessions that you can't control.

You were not meant to keep the pain of

broken promises, self-defeating thoughts –

the past, the unknown future, self-hatred

should-haves, could-haves, would-haves,

and want-tos –

You were meant to forgive yourself

and you have that permission ...

Prayer for Our Daughters

Creator, please

hold her in your arms

as she struggles

to define who she is –

Please help her to

realize that she is

a precious creation,

deemed fit in your eyes

not to be hit by the minds

of the spiritually oppressed

who never learned to respect themselves,

let alone a woman who gives life.

Please help her to take the first step

that is so hard to take but so necessary to

live and love, and please teach her worth.

Please help her to find the people she needs

to help her get back on her path,

the very one that she strayed from because

she may have put another before herself.

Please help her to fill her shoes

with new baby steps and her heart with the

gift of seeing beauty without violence –

And to see the beauty in this moment,

as she struggles to regain something humanity has lost

or perhaps didn't even know she lost –

Creator help her –

Dogs of my Childhood

Poopsi, Big Red, Hobo, Cinnamon

Hungry   cold   wanting to save them

Loving dogs, cold wet noses

Loves of my childhood

Warm shivering bodies

Next to mine

Mittens surrounding

Dogs' paws, legs, tummies

Trying to warm them up

Even for a few short minutes

They will know love from a child

To help them through the cold night

Poopsi –

Her cold nose twitched in the air

Her tummy felt like cold metal, she looked at me

I could not save her

Another dog bit her

Her entrails slowly freezing to the ground

Blood pooling around her cooling body

I knelt by her side and told her I loved her

Told her I was sorry, told her she was going to

Heaven to see all the other dogs

And jesus too and that I would miss her –

I cried, and frost grew on my eyelashes

The snot began to flow

I ate the other half of the sandwich

I saved for her

But I could not save her

She took her last breath

Eyes glazed over

Tongue hanging out the side of her mouth

Eyes like snowflakes

Falling before me

It was peanut butter and jelly

Emily and Dickonson

(Photograph of a bear and a girl on a bed {Bear's perspective})

I am a broken bear

Not even a real bear

I don't speak English

I don't speak Bear

I understand English

But not Bear

My owner taught me well

It is hot in here

How long do we have to sit

Will I get my salmon leftovers

I   want   to   bite   her   head   off

I   want   to   bite   his   head   off

Sitting like this hurts my ass bone

Control myself   control myself

It hurts to sit like this

Even though the bed is soft

My girl doesn't say much

Just cries into my fur

Wipes her snot on my coat

She wants to be a writer

She doesn't want to get married

She always looks at herself in the mirror

She says I am the only one who

Loves and understands her

I want to bite her head off

My girl's name is Emily

She calls me Dickonson

She is a broken girl

Not even a real girl

I am a broken bear

Not even a real bear

We are posing for a

Photographer

Not even a real photographer

Bad Day Metaphors

My life is a bowl

Of cold Cream of Wheat

Lumpy, bumpy,

Dehydrated, cold

Stuck to the spoon

My life feels like

A dog chasing its tail

Round and round I go

Like a birth-control wheel

Where it stops everyone

But me knows

Even the dog

Stops

My life is like three

Day-old bread

No one wants it

Except when it is free

Otherwise give

It to the fucking seagulls

Four Squares

I remember sitting in a bathroom painted white counting out the squares of toilet paper I was to use to clean myself. I remember the way I felt as I counted the squares feeling extremely guilty and like somehow the foster parents would know how much toilet paper I used. Thoughts ran through my mind like: They know how many squares there are on a roll and they will find out I used more than four squares. If I even use five squares they will find out and I will get hit with the belt. Being seven, scared, alone, lonely, anxious, and depressed didn't feel different to me; it was just the way things were.

What I remember the most is watching my little brother, who was five, being beaten with a fly swatter or belt or whatever the foster lady had in her hands. I remember his tears streaming down his face dripping off his jawline and the way his little hand was in his mouth trying to stifle his cries. I remember how broken and unsure of the world he was as this lady we were bestowed to call "Auntie Sharon" whipped him for wetting his bed. I learned later in life why children wet their bed and he was just doing what kids usually do when they are taken from their mother.

Little Brother

I See You Cry

I Hear You

I Can't Do Anything

To Help You

The Memory Haunts Me

Little Brother

I've Thought Of That Day

So Long Ago

Wishing You Would Not

Wet Your Bed

This Is Not Your Fault Little Brother

For Wetting Your Bed

Little Brother

Please Don't Spill Your Milk

Again, Or We Can't Eat

They Will Take Our Food

And Give It To The Dogs

Again

Little Brother

Please Stop Crying

Or She Will Throw You

Outside Again

Which Isn't A Bad Place To Be

But Today It's Cold And Raining

Little Brother

Please Play Quietly

Or She Will Come

And Make Sure

We Are Quiet

Little Brother Get Up

Your Clothes Are Dirty

And She Will Hit You Again

Either With The Fly Swatter

Or Perhaps The Leather Belt

Or Maybe A Rolling Pin

Little Brother Don't Play With The Boy

The One Who Blames You For Everything

And Laughs When You Get Hit

Little Brother Wipe Those Tears Away

And I'll Hold You Till Mom Comes Back

Little Brother Please Don't…

Sitting in a Box (To My Teenager)

Sitting in a box

At the bottom of the world

Clenched hands

Squeezing the box

Wrinkling its solidity

The clock ticking

Miles of road

Behind the box

Without wheels

And I wonder

Had you turned left

And I right

Would I have met you?

Would we have had to pave a road?

Built a bridge?

Written the next passage?

Sitting in a box

At the bottom of the world

I see you struggle with a fairy tale

Does good prevail over evil?

I see you try to make sense of the world

In a world where the quiet ones are left behind

In a world where people are lost behind money

And time has no real value but the wrinkles

Show just how far they've travelled, but they don't see that

They see the expensive mirror in front of them and the wrinkles

Are secondary as they slather expensive embryo cream all over

And the more money you have the less your wrinkles matter

We talk about this and we wonder what is more important?

Why does it seem that assholes make it to the top of the shit pile?

As if we were all flies in a dance to live longer with the biggest pile of shit

We talk about the war within ourselves to be spiritual or material

And we are both struggling to make sense of it and how a game

Could take so much of our time and we figure we are hiding from the world

We talk about why Daddies leave and why Mommies drink and why people

hurt little children and what becomes of those children

and we talk about fate or perhaps chance or we wonder if it is both

and I can't tell you anything except what I believe, and you can make up your

own mind sitting in the box at the bottom of the world

Sitting in a box at the bottom of the world

Let Me sit with You in this box

We'll watch the world stumble

Tremble, and fail, succeed and fall

And we will quietly reflect about

How we can be a part of the world

And yet apart, with our own thoughts

Feelings, and emotions, sitting in this box

As the world thunders all around us and time

Continued and our spirits travelled

And we know we needed to pick up the fragments

But just not today, but someday is good enough

For us to begin our journey as peacemakers

For today, we can sit in this box

At the bottom of the world

And watch the rain fall

And we can be rain too

A Splinter

An undying splinter of hope embedded in my heart and essence,
wanting and hoping heaven on earth exists amid the chaos;
a sliver of sanctuary ... within your embrace and desperation rears.
I am overwhelmed by the hairline fractures that begin to appear.
My erected walls of self-preservation become possible to penetrate
and I am standing on the edge again, shivering and afraid ...

The days quickly scorch by never quite melting the past,
My cloaks and daggers devoid of a clandestine closet.
Needing to believe, wanting to believe in fairy tales –
as I did before – as a child – reading all alone,
books clenched in my hands, stories vying in my head,
taking me away from it all; keeping me from
jumping off the edge toward freedom and sanity ...

Snowflakes bear witness to many a love's first kisses,
in a million places tonight and mine is no more
than one snowflake, melting without a footprint.
And yet ... I want to believe in fairy tales as
I did before as a child – reading all alone.
I want to believe I can overcome it all
like a sparrow ensnared in the moment she began,
finding sustenance and asylum-surviving the polar freeze,
 – a sliver of hope embedded in her heart ...

Lady Antiqua

She clambers into the darkened parlour, her daily nighttime lover,

sits at the bar so she may bear first witness to the birth of temporary love.

Noxious, familiar fumes of stale ale, both past and present,

assail her nostrils and burn her eyes and she feels like the freak she knows she is.

She never drinks before 6 p.m., except for today on her anniversary.

She's been alone 6 years, 351 days, 23 hours, and 54 minutes.

She orders the cheap, mind-numbing, bottom-of-the-barrel pale ale –

somehow remaining to be deceivingly effervescent, like her.

The gradation from light to dark consumes and justifies her fears –

she is the lost fairy tale princess; she is the loner waiting and

waiting for her prince to appear at the thrust of midnight with a black rose

or perhaps he may just drop from the sky onto her lap and rigorously shake her awake.

She thinks to herself what an intoxicatingly, dangerous last-call dream

to even beg for attention – quite unusual, insane, and sassy, she thinks.

She slowly sucks on her filtered second-rate cigarettes generating a death cloud,

staring and studying her, kumquat-hued, crinkled, creased fingertips.

And can't remember when she last felt the thunderstruck voice of love's whip entice her, daring her to push far and push hard and to grasp and reach for it blindly;

she's forgotten how to bat her lashes and caress her lips with her tongue.

What a life, what a quagmire to try and sneak up on love from behind,

like a bird flying north to purposely perish in the snow, alone, frozen, and unfulfilled.

She shivers and cringes at the lonely-decrepit-tarnished-broken-antique "ism" she is,

thunderstruck by the wrinkles that have crept and settled along her border

and made themselves invisible in the sepia-stained beer parlour encasing her in the wrong time.

Deep lines assault her in the unforgiving fluorescent spit of light and truth;

she can no longer hide from her lifetime stalker – age – who sets wrinkles in stone.

She gathers her wits and holds onto the bathroom sink hoping, begging, and praying;

– Maybe, Just Maybe – she might be seeing things in the wrong luminosity?

Maybe reading into a broken crystal ball – aged, cracked and abused? Like her? –

with only traces that it was ever really what it was supposed to be.

But she can no longer tell – her stalker has set her once-supple mouth

into an angry downturned line of wrinkles and peeling skin.

She blinks and opens her eyes, open and blink, blindly hoping to? Transform or morph

into anything else but the tired image of what was once a vibrant, sought-after Goddess.

Now? Just a broken montage of an aged soul in a dirty, cracked, Murderous Mirror.

The harsh daylight just as unforgiving, truthful, unrelenting, and ruthless

and cruel like all the others who didn't have enough sense to lie, lie, lie to her.

She is no longer on anyone's sexual mind for she has repented, retreated, and greeted defeat

into her lonely world of cheap booze, sad songs, dollar-store wine glasses, and postcards

of places she's never been but has sent off to past sexual participants of her life.

She is aching, waiting, preparing for her one night in shining armour to materialize

who will realize that he has finally found the one thing he has searched for his entire life.

Then she can finally slip on her negligee bought five years ago in a drunken state of denial.

She realizes one can never be too old to dream and she replays the clouded moment in her head

when he finally finds her and offers what little of life he has left and declares love for eternity.

She is ageless in the dark and this is her power, that and alcohol-inducing romance.

Until then she will inhale and puff incessantly and drink for two or three – or maybe just her

as she has always done while waiting for her aged lover on his last legs and last liver, like her ...

Awakening Tiger

Her haunches slowly quiver

in expectation of the unknown.

She rises to fullness

and stretches her neck.

Takes a penetrating b -r -e- a- t- h

Her nose twitches.

Her ears, a gentle spasm

listening for signs of warning –

Her eyes unadjusted

to the overwhelming light.

Her mouth is parched

and her growl is fresh

and her tummy vacant ...

She finally   S

          T

          A

          N

          D

          S

HOME

W-indy days

W-hip the young

G-rass into submission

B-irds land and soar

S-oar and land

U-pon foliage

F-lora and fauna

F-ully clad in spring.

G-ophers peek

I-nquisitively, crafty

J-ust over the prairie hills

P-reened and shined

G-lossy in the sun

F-ur gently swaying

I-n the morning sunlight.

T-he sun slyly rises

G-reater than it all

P-ounding downward

W-ith absolution.

W-indy days

S-un eaten, shadowless ... my home.

I Don't Want To

I want to fall asleep

upon your shoulder

in the secure, warm hollow

next to your heart

and be lulled by your

breathing

just like this

and play our game

of what if

just how lonely

we realize

we would be.

I want to awaken

every morning

just like this

with your arm

threaded through mine

placed with care

as not to stir my sleep.

Just hold me close to you

as you do every night

while I sleep.

I want to see my son's face

when I tell him

cats can have six babies

dogs and cats don't talk

we are ninety percent water

and clouds don't really cry.

I want to see my daughter

in any colour dress

that she chooses

walk down any aisle

or path she chooses

if I can see

that she really, really will

be fine without me.

I want to see the day

when my son realizes

that a pimple won't and can't

destroy your life, that

adolescence was learning

for those later years

when I could

teach no more.

I want to see a million

more rainy days

and a million more sunsets

and be able to count

all the precious little drops

and memorize all the orange

canvas splatters

painting the horizon,

that highlight the work

of art that you are.

I want to feel the snow

land upon my nose

and feel its cold penetration

upon my waiting tongue

while you stand there

and watch with a smile

and that ghastly camera.

I want to take a billion

and one

pictures with my

photographic memory

and be able to share them

with you through

the canvas of my voice.

Just like this.

I want to plant tiger lilies

watch them rise

and marvel at the delicious orange

the matchless contours

from the petal of the stem

to the pinnacle of

the beautiful blossomed crown

as I do to you.

I want to plant an oak

and have age rings

surround my heart

to mark the years

I have sheltered

and protected you

from the essences of

humanity

like a broken heart

death of a childhood

I want to protect you

with my branches

my arms.

I want to feel the ocean air

gently caress my face

and tousle our hair

while you place your

hand upon mine.

I want to see the stars

every day of my life

and have you see

the same dazzling sky

while you rest your trust

upon my shoulders

and become the loved one

you never felt you were.

I want to be able to pat

the dog that sat on a chair

across from me

and just sit and wonder

what is he thinking?

as his head moves left

right, more right, left, centre

his tongue-wagging

drool-dragging mouth

closed until the next

doggy ponder

and I am grateful to

be in this very moment

because it means

I am not stuck in yesterday

And not worried about tomorrow.

I want to be able to

make a difference

in a homeless person's life

by asking their name

lending strength

and carefully repeating

the words of encouragement

I have had whispered

in my youthful ears.

I want to feel your soul

intertwined with mine

and not hang on to

the hands of time

with greedy, defeated fists

but be forever

grateful and satiated

in your life

just like now.

I don't want to feel the signs

of slowly losing my mind

from age-induced amnesia

and not be able to remember

you every morning

just like this.

I don't want to become ill

and leave you behind

and not see my GRAND

CHILDREN learn to walk.

I don't want to feel

sickness

yours or mine

and silently cry

while you or I fight

to stay together

I don't want to have

to prepare you for

my absence

or me for yours

I don't want to –

Letter to My Nine-Year-Old Self

I knew why you didn't want to go home. I knew just how lonely you were and how sad you felt every time someone made you feel like you were nothing and you believed them. I knew the words that were tossed around that hurt you very much but you really couldn't do anything about it except listen and put it in the back of your mind to think about at a later date. The words swirled around "Bitch like your mother! Stupid bitch! Good for nothing!" I knew how much those words hurt coming from a grandmother who you knew was not like any other grandmas that you read about in books. I can tell you now little girl that I am so sorry that even your grandmother was broken. Your grandmother was broken like an enduring ceramic doll. What must have happened to her to make her so hateful toward you? It is not your fault little girl. I know you believed it for most of your nine years on this planet.

I knew the way you would angrily mash and mesh your fingers together repeat over and over how much you hated God and how much you didn't care if he knew you hated him. I knew how you wished he would take your life for taking his name in vain and for swearing at him. I knew you sort of believed in something higher than yourself because it kept you alive. I knew how you just stared at yourself in the mirror repeating over and over that "God doesn't exist God doesn't exist God doesn't exist" daring God to strike you down and bring his worst because anything worse would be better than this you thought. I know you truly believed and felt that if there really was a God you would not have had to live and feel this way where you did not want to live anymore. I knew that the very first time that you thought about suicide was when you were nine. I knew you heard about it before as time passed in your small world you would hear "Uncle Leonard ... shotgun ... head ... couldn't do it anymore ... hung themselves ... drug overdose ... Auntie Donna ... eighteen ... shot herself in the head ... left her baby behind ..."

I knew how mad you were at a God who would take both your mom and dad away from you and let others sexually abuse you. I knew how disgusted you felt and how powerless you were to actually do anything about it. I knew about the sexual abuse in foster care. I knew about the sexual abuse on the reserve. I know you knew it wasn't right but what could you do at nine and I am sorry no one was there. Truly I am very sorry. I knew when you told someone about it for the very first time it was your grandmother. I knew how hard it was to gather the courage to tell someone that someone was hurting you especially to tell someone a huge secret and especially someone you were afraid of. I knew how relieved you were when you finally told someone and that it was not a secret anymore. I knew she slapped you and told you to quit lying. I knew she also blamed you for what happened. At nine, you heard it was your fault. I know you rolled these thoughts around in your head and wondered how it could be your fault. How could it be your fault? How could it be your fault? How could it be your fault? I knew you learned to run and hide. I knew it was safer in the dog house even in the rain. I am so sorry little one for such horrible behaviour. I am trying so hard not to hate her right now as I knew growing up you hated her. I don't hate her anymore and one day you won't anymore.

I knew that at nine you were hospitalized but they could not find anything wrong with you. I knew you wanted to stay at the hospital because the nurses and the doctors made you feel like you mattered and it truly seemed that they cared. I knew about the doctor who would bring you a Fruit and Nut bar every night for a month straight. I knew he would just sit by your bed and listen to you talk about nothing really. You even told him about your dog Hobo. I knew how you wished you could go home with the doctor who talked to you asked questions and listened. I know.

Sometimes you imagine even now the hospital experience being different. Perhaps you think that maybe just maybe you should have told about the sexual abuse. Maybe the doctor would have brought you home to live in his wonderful house and a Fruit and Nut Bar would be a tradition when you felt sad. I knew that you had depression at nine years old and that it would be OK if you could just have a month of people caring for you. I knew you felt you could make it through. I knew little girls went into the hospital and left and yet you still did not want to go home even when you could hear the little girls crying at night wanting to go home. You actually cried at night because you didn't want to go home. I knew how easy it was to fall asleep listening to the quietness of the empty hallways. Once in a while you would hear the squeak of a nurse's shoe as she did her rounds and you knew she would check on you too.

How lonely you must have been to be waiting for a few kind words and gentle touches from strangers when it should have been family that you felt the safest with. I am so sorry little girl for the lack of gentle loving touch for the lack of hugs for the lack of innocent kisses for the lack of kind words and for the lack of trust. I also knew that books and your mind took you away from all and that if it wasn't for books you probably wouldn't know anything outside of dysfunction. I knew your imagination took you away from the truth and brought you a temporary sense of safety. I knew that you knew that there was something more and different but what you didn't know was how to get there especially since you were too small to leave the reserve. You knew one day that you would for sure try to get away – if you were still alive.

I know that you never felt valued and your sense of self was not really yours. I knew that you could mould your personality to be whatever anybody else liked or wanted. If they liked a clean house I knew you would clean it just to hear those few kind words of what an amazing cleaner you were which meant you had some value. Those few kind words would hold you over and make you feel good for a few moments until the next time you moulded yourself into something somebody else wanted you to be. I knew how you never said no to babysit for free because it meant that someone valued you for what you could do for them. I knew you felt that if they valued you for something you could do for them you could see through their eyes and value yourself for a little while because it meant you were something and something was better than nothing. I know some of the phrases used to describe you when you were nine were "a great help a great babysitter a great cleaner a good girl who listens a good dishwasher a good student" etc. I knew how great you were to others as long as you were doing something for them and some of those things were secrets.

I knew you knew how to disassociate but didn't realize that you were doing just that. You knew instinctively how to protect yourself and you knew how to pretend things did not happen. I knew you basically lied to yourself and others just so you could protect yourself. I know you used to pretend your life was different from what it was and that you felt if people knew others were touching you in a bad way that they would think you were bad and not offer you any kind words or they would not let you do things for them anymore that would solicit those kind words. I know that you needed those kind words to be able to get through your life. I am so sorry for humanity little girl. The chain of events that led to you standing and looking in the mirror hating yourself and cursing God I knew about that too.

I know that school was a place that felt safe for you and it was a place where if you excelled you could and would get those kind words. I know Mr. Perry was one of the main reasons that you loved school so much. I know you wished he was your dad and not just your teacher. I know how much his kind words of encouragement made you feel like you may actually matter in the world and you did matter in this world especially when he smiled at you and seemed genuinely proud of your accomplishments. I know how safe happy and loved you felt at school because no one knew where you came from and what others thought of you. You could invent another little girl who did have real birthdays with cake presents love and plenty of real hugs and innocent kisses. I know at school you could be that normal little girl you read about in books and perhaps that was God's gift to you to have a childlike mind perspective and ideals so that you could survive to have your own children one day where hugs flowed freely and those three little words "I love you" would be tossed around like you actually had that family tradition.

I know you had to practice those three words that you only heard when your mom was around and I know that you told your dogs that you loved them all the time. I know they were your best friends and I know they saw you cry. I know you talked to them and believed they listened and maybe just maybe carried your words to the angels who watched over children. Perhaps the words were even passed on to the Creator which is why your soul always believed in goodness. I know they licked your tears and listened when you told them how sad and confused you were. I know how special dogs were to you. Your dogs valued you and you wished they could speak to you and tell you what to do what to feel and where to go. I know you played house and school with your dogs and I knew how much it hurt when they were starving. I know how you would sneak food out to them and pat their heads as they ate. I know how much it hurt when one of the dogs didn't come home and how you would imagine them dying alone. I knew at nine you wished that if they were dead that it had been quick and painless. I know how sane those dogs kept you in a world that you couldn't make sense of and the only goodness in the summer was the hours spent playing with the dogs under the hot sun.

I know how you could never live in the moment because you were always afraid afraid of the past afraid of the future afraid of footsteps at night and afraid of footsteps in the day. I knew how much you wished you could fly so you could always be safe whenever someone was hurting you. I knew how much you hated your life and how much you wanted to be loved to feel like you belonged and to be valued for being just you. I know you knew those words from reading but never truly felt them consistently like the people in books. I knew you knew that life wouldn't always be this sad, and I know you knew that you would get out but patience to a nine-year-old is definitely more than a virtue. I know at nine you knew what virtue meant because you read it in books and wondered how it even applied to you if you didn't have value to anybody anyway. I know you always felt different different from other kids who could laugh freely ... those ones that you somehow knew you weren't afraid. I know you wished you were them and a lot of your time was spent daydreaming about being someone else other than yourself. I know you always questioned why you were you and they were them.

I know you wished you could take ballet and have pretty pink ballet slippers and I know you wanted to play guitar and have someone who loved you drive you to your lesson like the kids in books and I know you would never complain like the kids in books. I know one day that any negative things words people places things would someday be replaced with things that felt safe to you and that one day you would be in control of your world. I know you knew that you would get out but you didn't know how.

I know you had no toys or books of your own except for one stuffed bear that your mom sent from India or perhaps Toronto and I knew how you tried to connect with her through your mind heart and soul whispering the nine-year-old mantra "Please Mom … come get me … I'll be good. I promise. Please Mom … come and get me … I'll be good … I promise … Please …" I know you never questioned her love for you and that she was never around long enough to actually allow you to trust anyone at all even her.

I can tell you little girl that you are a wonderful little girl whose imagination brought you to better places places you read about in books places you saw on the one channel on Sunday nights. I can tell you that there are angels who take care of children and sometimes they are in human form and sometimes they don't even know how much they saved and influenced your life … until you tell them. I know you would tell them someday through your healing journey and through your words.

I can see you now in my mind's eye sitting on the porch stairs hair braided and thinking, thinking, always thinking. I can tell you just how beautiful your soul was is and will be and about the love you had for Mother Earth; it far surpassed the love you had for yourself. Perhaps you have always had a mother under your feet whispering in your ear and hair on a breezy day when you were again thinking unlike a nine-year-old should. I can tell you just how strong you were and how that strength would be shared with your own children one day.

I know you missed your mom every single day and I know you never knew if and when you would ever see her again and I knew that was a very scary feeling that lived in the bottom of your stomach every day. I knew that sometimes you cried because you thought she was dead, because she was gone for years. I know how much you hoped and called to the universe as well as trying to reach her telepathically if that was even possible but I knew you read about it in some book. I know that you never told your mom about the abuse because the words to describe it were too hard to say without feeling that maybe just maybe it could be partially your fault and maybe she would stop loving you. I know you also didn't tell her because those dirty words that rolled off your tongue the first time you told were still stuck somewhere in your being where you put them. You knew your mom would not hit you for it but you didn't want to scare your mom away so you told her things that made her happy. I know you pretended to be OK so your mom could pretend everything was OK too.

I know you carried a lot on your little shoulders and I knew it was a struggle to survive. I know that you kept things inside and that you knew how to disassociate and go away from the moment and live in a cloud where time didn't matter and where being human didn't hurt like a nightmare come true. I know that was your safe space and then you could and would not even bother to remember it and if the idea came to visit you knew how to chase it back into the dark forest in your brain. I know you were just surviving. I know.

I can tell you that your mom loved you with her entire broken being then again it seemed you always knew that and it was her love that kept you hanging on. I can tell you that she wished she could have been like the moms in books. She loved reading books just like you did ... just like you did because she escaped in books as well. I know you wanted to be with her with your entire being and that she loved you with hers but she couldn't even take care of herself so how could she take care of you?

I can tell you that she had too many bad things happen to her in her life: that she drank alcohol to numb the pain and to forget the past. I know the only future she saw was where she was going to get the next bottle from but oh how she loved you. She wished you could have been with you like the families in the books she read. I can tell you that your dad loved you but couldn't care for you either because he was in survival mode. He was also recovering from his past just like your mom. I can also tell you that those males that hurt you were very very damaged themselves and that none of it was ever your fault. I can tell you that you will become a great person with lots of insight because of all the experiences. I can tell you that your grandmother was also very damaged and that if she could do it all over again she would have been strong in a different way instead of keeping the truth of the past at bay with the rosary and a braid of Sweetgrass. I can tell you that every thought and experience you had has shaped you into an absolute empath. I can tell you I am sorry for humanity and that I love you.

Summer Kisses

I crawl out from under my unparalleled agate rock with cherry

blossom polka-dotting my greying hair.

My lonely hibernation is over, and I smile, steadfast, and maybe this is

the year I fall hard and fast

headlong into a summer astral travel – awake and vibrant and not want

for any other in my sacred space.

I search desperately for my elusive one, who will not be afraid of

change and not be afraid to swim

into the sea under a full moon, stripped of his ego in the intimate hush

of night – him and I …

He would not be afraid to arrange himself on my star blanket bursting

with unspoken hopes,

unspoken expectations of virtuous pleasure, and gaze at the stars

without the encapsulation

of time limiting our interaction, our intimacy and just be – just be in

the moment with only me.

The sun plants copper-brown kisses upon my face, my arms, my legs,

my shadows

and I realize just how breakable am I – I realize I am not here, nor

there, not anywhere

but in a Milky Way of moments that I must choose with a free and

lucid mind so that I may

one day remember what it was like to run across the sand barefoot and

in the clutches of love,

to feel the reckless abandon of the first touch and to never question the

sanity of my need for love,

leading me down a twisted path of desire, leaving me aching for more

time to live in my old age.

All I know is that I am not with him at this very moment when it truly

would be the

difference between sanity and insanity, loneliness and fulfillment,

between lust and love,

and I know somewhere under the coverlet of the sky, he is wishing he

knew where to find me …

In a field of emerald and fearless dandelions, summer is dressing up for

me and for my elusive one,

and the tiger lilies shout "he loves You he loves You not" as I float by

through the field untouched by

ownership, where it is liberating to be just who I am – just me …

I place a delicate crimson-copper petal upon my tongue of distant

memories and remember just how

they used to taste (when I was a little girl dreaming of womanly things

I would never know for sure),

just how sweet and innocent should they taste? I recollect and regroup

in the tall grasses reminiscing

about how many times I have thought that I have been in love and the

summer delicately disappears

leaving behind many unanswered questions and the daggers in my

heart that I hide from the world …

I feel the insignificance of my memories of just how small and

cherished I feel as I say

goodbye to the sun who kissed me, caressed me, shined and showered

me for seventy-seven days.

I realize just how small I am in a field filled with nature's delicacies,

truths, and dares

as I contemplate the meaning of my ability to love with reckless

abandon and shameless lust

and my ability to distinguish love from lust – and I am humbled and

brought to my knees ...

I let the sun kiss my face, my eyelids, my soul that slowly fades and

vanishes leaving me in the field

just as I am and accepts the need for me to dream of the perfect life

with a soulmate who complements

me and doesn't leave my heart in a cold dark room, quivering with the

unknown.

IF Mother could have spOken…

I never meant to leave you my children; I was trying to run from the storm that raged and fought inside of me. It hurts so bad to know that I left pain and confusion in your path.

From the first time I had been touched as if my body was that of a woman when I was a tiny girl. I have tried… to run from their sins, but it's not possible to run from myself. I tried so hard to stay with your dad for as long as I could but… The storm that raged inside me was fiery anger and it wanted to get out somehow, anyway, it could. I turned to the bottle for comfort and I finally felt relief from this life.

Your dad wanted me to quit so bad with his love for me, but even his love couldn't calm the devil that chased me since I felt their dirty hands upon me, trying to tell me they were god's messengers.

*If they were messengers than I thought that god was sure one sick son of a *****!*

But now that I found a medicine that could take away all the pain, I can't seem to stop, even as I look at your tiny faces. I felt only shame when I walked away. I felt the shame I felt all my life and it felt normal to be buried in this shame. I let shame embrace me, mould me, and take me away and I'd follow 'cause if I veered off the path toward righteousness others told me I was acting too high-class and would offer me a swig of cheap rotgut whisky. If I was already down, not one person in sight would even offer me a quarter for my next bottle. But you my babies, you were so pure, I wanted to protect you, but I didn't know how I was going to do that with all the craziness going on around me. I figured that if at least I could show you and plant a seed within your minds that somehow you could make it out of here no matter what happened. I wanted to plant the idea of a pure love… A love so huge that you would one day know that I did die for you… So that you could go on. I wanted you to analyze MY life and do everything in your power not to give up like me. You would say to me, and I know this MY girl, "MOM, you never gave up, you did your best with what you had and what you knew," but I tell you I think I knew deep down in MY deadened spirit that I never had a chance but I did get a chance to have three wonderful babies.

And having you kids and seeing you for the first time was the only time I never felt dirty.

How could there be anything dirty about

You kids who were so skinny and helpless?

I lacked nutrition to have nine-pound kids

that the white women were having

But MY babies were the cutest and the quietest

Even the nurses were in awe of MY five-pounders

I told them, "I pack light," they stood there

wondering whether to laugh or take out Canada's food guide.

Geometry

I never knew where Uganda was

Or maybe will never physically know

I was never good at geometry

Philosophy my cheap box of wine

Nor psychology at any time

Never understood sociology,

Or the nuances that defined a society.

All I know is I never look people in the eye

As a sign of respect to my Elders

But in modern society it is considered a weakness

Or perhaps one is shifty and dishonest.

What's worse? Being disrespectful

Or being considered a coward?

How do you bridge the cultural gap?

Without changing into two people?

One brown with a frown and one white and uptight?

Not wanting to pick up a used baton

And travel a bumpy unknown road

Where many others' spiritual bones

Lay scattered among the forgotten road.

Heroes? Or people who have lost it all?

It's all about perspective

And what colour your skin is.

I was never good at geometry,

Couldn't tell you where Uganda was or is,

Or crunch numbers and save nickels

But let me tell you what I do know:

You should never hit a woman

Or call her derogatory names

a life-giver within her body

bringing forth new life.

You should never oppress a child

Or tell them they are stupid

And limit their chances to thrive

And live a peaceful life.

You should never hurt the people you love

Intentionally to the point where love

Becomes frozen

And you're a world apart

Yet still close enough to feel the sorrow.

You should never be afraid to cry big

cleansing tears and mournful wails

leaving the past to yesterday and the future

to the unknowing.

Live in this moment and notice everything

And don't be afraid to fly,

Spread your tarnished wings

Fly higher than the past ...

Forgiveness

By the grace of the Creator do I continue to walk this Earth and breathe this air, thoughts rolling through my head like dry tumbleweeds on an old movie set, rhyme and reason, I say. One additional wrong step and I may have been one of the Missing and Murdered Indigenous Women. I may have taken my own life, intentionally or unintentionally. I may have been stuck inside addiction, inside my head, almost dead.

Suicide, drug addiction, alcoholism, depression, and colonialism run through my blood, passed on through cell memory, past events, DNA, history, stories ... And yet here I sit writing what's in my head, heart, soul, and body, knowing that it is all not in vain but in my veins.

MY MOM drank her pain away trying to chase away the demons of her past and keep them at bay with fiery poison coursing through her veins, making her world blurry and pain free, so she was drunk more often than she was sober. She was born around the time prohibition was lifted and her parents, my grandparents, couldn't take care of her either. I don't remember meeting them, but apparently they met us a few times way back when, when there weren't any cellphones, house phones were for the rich, and a car a luxury that an alcoholic could not possibly afford with his or her fire-water habit. Besides, back then, according to MY MOM, "Who would hire an Indian?"

MY MOM was sexually abused since she could remember, which was from about the age of four, and raped at twelve by a man of the church. When she told me her stories, she didn't tell it like it happened to her. She told it like it was a character from a book she was reading. I wasn't raised by MY MOM. I was raised by my colonial-kissed grandmother who had each foot in a different culture.

My grandmother was born in 1911 in a time when major changes affected people with brown skin. If I think about it, 1867 would have been when "Indians" were given numbers and today we still have those ten-digit numbers. Kind of like the Holocaust victims, only we were being eradicated spiritually, mentally, and emotionally through strategic acts, both conscious and unconscious, of perceived-superior thinking.

Sources for "An 'Indian' Never Dies Peacefully"

"At least 4,000 aboriginal children died in residential schools, commission finds." *National Post,* January 3, 2014. Last updated January 25, 2015. http://news.nationalpost.com/2014/01/03/at-least-4000-aboriginal -children-died-in-residential-schools-commission-finds.

Royal Canadian Mounted Police. "Missing and Murdered Aboriginal Women: A National Operational Overview." Reports, research, and publications. Last modified May 27, 2014. http://www.rcmp-grc.gc.ca/en /missing-and-murdered-aboriginal-women-national-operational-overview.

Acknowledgments

"An 'Indian' Never Dies Peacefully" was published in *ricepaper*. Thanks to the editors.

There are many, many people in my life who have been catalysts for me for the healing that I needed to do, many people who are still a part of my life today, and of course future souls that I will also meet, thank you too ... Thank you Catriona and Cecily for the patience and the time, energy, and eyes to read and edit my work; because at times, I know you even wondered how the world could be so cruel. Thank you both because it is now ready to be shared in the universe.

Thank you Talonbooks for the belief in me when I didn't even believe in myself, you were another one of those healing catalysts, and you continue to shine the light on important issues and great writers. Thank you for your continuous support for my work and thank you to the dogs as well that always calmed my nervous energy for sure! And thanks also to Leslie S. for the beautiful cover.

Thank you Christina H. for all the wonderful healing love and light you share with the world and with me as well!

Thank you to all the beautiful souls I work with at MCFD. You'll never know the impact of heart you have on the people you work with, especially when you open your mind and heart and use the past as a gauge for families and their struggle and for helping them, instead of harming them. Thank you Stacia J. for all your guidance and belief in me and for your words of support and encouragement.

Thank you to the Canada Council and the BC Arts Council for their financial support.

Thank you to Ania W. for stepping up for me, standing for me and for believing in me with your beautiful presence and curious soul.

Thank you Daisy K. for walking with me as a fellow woman in a crazy world and helping me to plant my feet next to yours when I needed it.

Thank you Terri B. for your acceptance, your love and caring and your ability to "get" my jokes that are definitely one-offs in some circles! And thank you for your kind, loving heart.

Thank you Stacey Q. for you friendship, belief in me, and your willingness to talk me off the ledge of insanity in a world you seem to have figured out or maybe just appear to have figured ... I love that!

Thank you Sara P. for your infectious laugh that startles me into unexpected happiness and your wonderful listening skills!

Thank you Ian P., my teacher in elementary and junior high who offered a gentle healing space and who taught me to believe in myself with his guitar and songs about geometry, geology, and even math.

Thank you my children, Tan, Taylor, Kuna, Kiyano, Miya, for giving me the love and the silly faces that I will ever need in a lifetime (but don't stop). You continue to inspire me and to teach me about life every single day. Thank you for choosing me to be your mother when you were deliberating whether to come back here at all! You chose me so you could learn as well and one day you can share with me that lesson ... My hearts ... Thank you LD for being so accepting, loving, kind, and a miracle worker with broken spirits and for all the healing that you have placed in the universe, especially with me. You will always be my saviour.

Thank you Lynn M. for the use of your precious space to complete my writing and also thank you for your ear when life threw dirt at my fan ... One day I may need one of yours so I can throw it at the people who go over thirty kilometres an hour in a park zone. (Not your ear, I'd throw the fan.)

Thank you to my brothers Hank and JJ for being so kind, loving, and teachable as well as teaching me things. The importance of siblings is beyond measure ... I love the journey, the lessons, and the laughs and the fishing expeditions without fishing rods. They both make dreamy bannock!

Thank you Sophia R. for your openness, your laughter, and your want to do better for the children you work with and for being a support when I needed it.

Thank you Grace W. for your kindness, love, understanding and for always helping bail out my boat with me and my children in it. You have stopped us from sinking many times and you are due soon for a haircut!

Thank you to all the Indigenous writers and "pavers" for paving the way for me and also for others starting the writing path, may they become strong word warriors! Thank you Jónína K, Joanne A, Janet R, Russell W, Lee M, Bev. S, Richard W, Vera M, Gary G, Richard V, Rosa and Melvin J, and many other Indigenous writers and performers who inspire and ignite to create more word warriors.

Thank you Ariadne S. for the wonderful space you create and momentum you carry, and for your caring, compassionate soul that moves people across all spectrums of the rainbow.

Thank you to Auntie Brenda J., who has been my mom when my mom could not and thank you for making the world a better place by being a role model of what it's like to achieve a state of "normal." Your courage, strength, beauty, and intelligence are leaving ripples in the world.

Thank you Margaret M. for creating healing ripples in the world and for creating space for others to push forward beyond the scope of acceptance of pain and poverty.

Thank you Nat K. for your love, laughter, acceptance, and healing sisterhood that is in abundance even if our worlds are far apart because we are busy in our own lives … I know if I needed you, you would come … Thank you Stacia J. for the healing light you bring to this world with your grace, beauty, lived experience, and the support you offer our people in a broken world.

Thank you Garry M. and his mom for starting me on my writing path through your acceptance, encouragement, and your ability to see beyond … Thank you Tina M. for your acceptance, love, and humour to see beyond the impossible, and helping others to grow through the art of shared storytelling.

Thank you Ron A. for being straight with me and always pushing me forward with words a father would say to their daughter, like "All it is is willpower," and me saying, "Whaaaaaatttttttt?, seriously though."

Thank you to Cristina S, for your love, kindness, acceptance, and for attending my readings and wholeheartedly caring for my Miss Miya and me and for giving me time to create.

Thank you Mom, Dad, and Kokum for the wherewithal and the courage and the mistakes that shone a light on the future for me. Thank you for being there as much as you could be and I know you would have done things differently seeing beyond the trauma of colonial history. If you were here, Kokum, I would have forced you to take a hug and done it every time I saw you so you would be comfortable with it and know it doesn't really hurt and isn't scary.

Thank you Nanay and Tatay for caring for Miss Miya even when you're sick and thank you for making sure her clothes are ironed and matched because I can't see in the dark when she's sleeping! Thank you for loving her with all your heart!

Thank you to all the readers, writers, listeners, and supporters of Indigenous writers and thank you for walking on the journey with us … walking a mile in our moccasins! Thank you for your open minds and hearts!

Thank you Guarino A. for the laughs, the healing, the openness to learn new things, the patience it takes to play Barbies with Miya. Thank you for the support with my writing and my job and thank you for feeding all the animals! And thank you for taking on this new role that requires us to heal together through trial and error and now after seven years, it's way easier … Practice makes almost perfect … And thank you Creator for always putting forth whatever it is I needed in front of me in the most unusual ways possible, yes you definitely have a sense of humour, that's where "the joke's on you" came from. Thank you for always picking me up …

WANDA JOHN-KEHEWIN, Cree/Métis from Kehewin, Alberta, has studied criminology, sociology, Aboriginal studies, and creative writing. She uses writing as a therapeutic medium to understanding and responding to the near-decimation of First Nations cultures, languages, and traditions. She has been a part of World Poetry and their radio show as a co-host on Co-op Radio, and performed at numerous readings throughout British Columbia's Lower Mainland. Her work is raw, and her honesty reflects the amount of suffering the Ancestors of the past have endured. She gives a voice to her mother, who was never heard. She credits her children as her vehicle to healing and wanting to understand colonization and its effects. Her first book of poetry, *In The Dog House*, was published by Talonbooks in 2013.